PSYCHOANALYSIS AND MANAGEMENT

PSYCHOANALYSIS AND MANAGEMENT
THE TRANSFORMATION

David Gutmann
with Oscar Iarussi

Translated from the French by Matthieu Daum

KARNAC

LONDON   NEW YORK

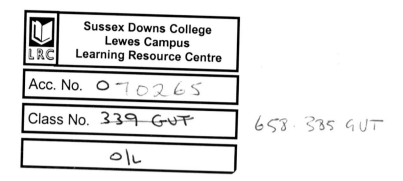
First published in 1999 in Italian:
La Trasformazione: Psicoanalisi, desiderio e management nelle organizzazioni
by Edizioni Sottotraccia.

French edition published in 2000:
La Transformation: Psychanalyse, désir et management by l'Hermès

This English edition published in 2003 by
H. Karnac (Books) Ltd.
6 Pembroke Buildings, London NW10 6RE

British Library Cataloguing in Publication Data

A C.I.P. for this book is available from the British Library

ISBN 1 85575 992 6

Edited, designed, and produced by The Studio Publishing Services Ltd,
Exeter EX4 8JN

Printed in Great Britain

10 9 8 7 6 5 4 3 2 1

www.karnacbooks.com

CONTENTS

ACKNOWLEDGEMENTS

This book was conceived thanks to a meeting with Oscar Iarussi initiated by Pina Labellarte.

Amongst the Italian friends that I would like to thank are Salvatore Cotugno, Mario de Pasquale, Vito Volpe, and Maria-Giovanna Garuti of ISMO in Milan.

I shall not forget, of course, Jacqueline Ternier-David and the whole Praxis International team, as well as all my colleagues at the International Forum for Social Innovation.

Special thoughts go to my parents—Haim and Sarah—thanks to whom the past was able to give birth to the present, and to my sons—Michael, Raphael, and Benjamin—who made the future spring up and to whom I feel linked with a tender and tumultuous complicity.

The emotion that we have felt along the way is dedicated, before anyone else, to my wife Annie and to Maria-Theresa, Oscar's spouse.

WARNING

This book was devised during the summer of 1996 and, to remain loyal to its content, no real additions or amendments have been carried out since in the actual book.

The author reveals the importance of the "here and now", and demonstrates the predominance of the diagnostic at the expense of the prognostic.

By the time the diagnostic is sufficiently unveiled, the rest just follows.

PREFACE

I read the French edition of David Gutmann's book *La Transformation: Psychanalyse, Désir et Management* in August 2000. He reveals in the book some aspects related to his tragic familial history, of which I was totally unaware, although I have known him for several years.

At that time, the Tate Modern had just opened and in one of its north-west rooms, it had on display a gigantic photograph by Hannah Collins called "In the course of time II". It was a picture of the Jewish cemetery in Warsaw in 1994: amid trees that had grown among the neglected graves, one, a little less slanting than the others' bore a name: Anna GUTMANN. Having seen this I made a promise to myself to bring David to this room in order to show him, without having the need to say it directly, that I had read his book and that I appreciated his approach of simultaneously mingling his thoughts about his work and his private life. This showed that he was applying to himself what he was saying to his clients: know how to manage the inescapable uniqueness of your personality, at work as well as in your daily life.

Some months later, while he was in London, I took him to visit the Tate. The picture was no longer there. Doubtless, a "coincidence"!

I met David Gutmann through some work he did with one of the institutions he talks about in this book, but I began to work with him only after I had taken on responsibilities in a perfectly English company. This honourable institution, whose creation dates back to the nineteenth century, has had to go through multiple changes including nationalization after World War II, privatization during Thatcher's years, acquisition—slightly rough—by an American company from the heart of the South gripped by the world conquest demon, followed less than two-years later by resale as a whole to a French company—nationalized to boot—a supreme snub!

But why on earth work with a French adviser on leadership in such a context?

Was it in order to be certain of distancing myself enough from my daily responsibilities, which were sometimes rather absorbing? It seems that this was the case without doubt, even though underneath the perfect professionalism of my British colleagues, and their humour always tinged with a touch of self-derision, one can still feel their great difficulty in revealing their true attraction to the gambling aspect of business. Also, through their benevolence, which is often combined with a slight amusement to the attraction I happened to have for great ideas, some of which are not always followed up and implemented, they were always perfectly able, in a very civil way, to get me to assess options which would always have something slightly strange about them, or look different.

Was this choice to allow me to better manage the complexities that sometimes agitated the French institution, to which I was accountable, when they began to develop an awareness of the role of shareholders in an English public service enterprise? This was possibly the case, even though the former was preoccupied with the management of it's own transformation on the continent and, perhaps due to the distance between London and Paris, I always enjoyed this kind of support, strong but distant enough, which allowed me never to be diverted from pursuing my objectives on this side of the Channel.

Was it to better manage the anxiety which happens to assail any manager and to prevent him from the consequences of the "murderous projections" he can generate? Probably, though human relations here always seemed to me much more urbane—at least apparently—than on the other side of the Channel, where the longing for a "Grand Soir" or a revolution inevitably agitates the souls every twenty five or thirty years, i.e. just enough to mark each generation.

Was it to learn how "to live and not to survive" as Chapter Two of the book invites us to do? Certainly, even if the condition of the "Chairman" of a well-known and reputable company in London has but remote connections with a survival situation—especially if he is lucky enough to be there with his family who can daily appreciate the opportunities of discovery and surprise offered by this town through the daily contact with so many similarities and differences!

I have also learnt with no doubts, to move from "the wish to implement a plan" to "the desire to pursue the journey" of the transformation of a company according to David Gutmann's words in this book.

But finally, I think that our collaboration allowed me to be a little bit less unbearable for my colleagues which, if all things are taken into consideration, is a result that cannot be totally ignored.

I do hope so and for this reason at least, I invite you to read this book.

B. Lescoeur
Chairman of London Electricity Group (1999–2002)

FOREWORD

This book centres on the work and world of ideas of David Gutmann, a consultant to institutions and organizations. This is a man who personifies social, political and spiritual processes, which are central to any definition of the twenty-first century. David Gutmann, a man for all seasons, is passionate about his work and life in general. For the book, an Italian journalist, Oscar Iarussi, a man of letters, interviews him. Although I have never met Oscar Iarussi, I remain grateful to him for his sheer determination to remain a faithful listener, able to contribute, echoing David Gutmann's evocations in bringing parallel associations and analogies from his own personal experiences. After each meeting he retires to reflect and writes his thoughts at the end of each chapter. A rich dialogue emerges between the two of them and a terrific tension is present almost all the time.

When I was first asked about writing the introduction to this book I felt both excited and thrilled. I also felt privileged and honoured to have been entrusted with this intellectual and experiential challenge.

I thought that this would also give me the chance to reflect and to think of my own journey of self-discovery and transformation since I first met David, who is partly, unwittingly, responsible for my own emotional growth.

I have known Professor Gutmann for a long time, our working association has been a long and complicated journey since it has gone through many and various spheres and layers of work with many "zigzags", until eventually a friendship emerged.

I first met David Gutmann in 1988 as the consultant of my "Small Study Group". At the time I was a member at the annual Group Relations Conference on Authority, Leadership and Organization attending the meeting of the so-called "Leicester" Conference. I am not sure how many of this book's readers are familiar with the dynamics of institutions and organizations. The conference aims at the learning, in an experiential way, of issues to do with personal authority and leadership in different contexts.

Those who go to a conference for the first time in their lives experience an initial sense of intimidation, fear, and some creeping anxiety further confirmed by others familiar with the conference, who have been before, who solemnly "warn" the newcomers with statements that whereas "It is an experience impossible to describe" and/or "You just have to go and experience it for yourself" always marked with a threatening and almost menacing quality, as "Life won't be the same afterwards". So, in a way it is predictable that the new attendees enter this unknown territory of new experiences overtaken by an impending sense of doom. At times all these feelings and sensations increase to reach almost panic proportions.

My first encounter with David Gutmann, had a quasi-therapeutic feeling when I was confronted with his sharp assertions. I felt so provoked by him that towards the end of the first week I wanted to leave; I thought his arrogance was beyond belief. He pushed me to my limits and later on when reflecting, I became aware that this was his way to make me act on my hidden resources, resources I had, but were not easily available to me. He had become the container of many of my projections, especially those concerned with hatred. That is what he calls confrontation leading to transformation, with most insightful interpretations.

Gutmann says: "My concept of *revelation* does not only include what is known as psychoanalytical *insight*, there is also an element of *input*, which can lead to an *output*. Revealing in order to transform, then. And an insight is not enough: what needs to be added is the shock of great violence that is the output".

As mentioned earlier I learnt about this from hard experience, feeling bruised, even wounded by David's sharp interpretations. They are the outcome of a potent combination of his perception and enormous sensibility, delivered with an almost sarcastic quality which at times is experienced as a brutal shock in a true confrontation with "the other" that it is later revealed as a part of oneself. From then on life for me was never the same.

From reading this book I became aware that David had himself experienced important events in 1988, such as his father's death and the ending of his psychoanalysis. I wonder now if these had, to some degree, sharpened his own sense of those around him.

In this book he candidly talks of his own family experiences, in that he could have felt not only a survivor, but also a replacement child, or even part of a replacement family with his father unable to grieve because of his survivor guilt. David opens himself up and shares with us his own areas of vulnerability which, if unprepared, are bound to appear.

He does not indulge in any feelings of being a survivor, on the contrary, his awareness of death and the importance of mourning are essential in the choice we all make of either live or survive. This consciousness makes it possible to live and to do the maximum possible between the beginning and the end.

Survivors are either those who succumb to revenge, bitterness and denial, or those who make the effort to generate activities of great creativity. This helps to break the cycle and it requires self-knowledge, never being taken for granted.

Survivor he is not, and he certainly wants to live his life to the full and to contribute as much as possible to the interests of the world. He is passionate about so many enterprises, including politics *per se*, applied institutions and organizations, chemistry, genocide, industrialization, spirituality, history, etymology, sociology, mythology, films, works of art, literature, philosophy and even the game of rugby is thrown in!

His important contribution to the understanding of the dynamics operating in institutions and organizations, is the innovation of the principle of transformation based on Bion's ideas which he then develops as the Transformation-Approach which, he believes, is full of common sense, where the struggle is on the transformation of the zigzag pathway, in the need to increase the "zig" and decrease the "zag".

Not only is the individual faced with the choice of either survival or transformation, but also the institutions.

For him it is essential that the interpretation must transform understanding into action, hence his coining of the word Transform-Action.

He tries to comprehend the world, at times taking the risk of being rather grandiose, and nothing seems to stop him from attempting enormous enterprises, in a rather quixotic way, with unexpected insights.

For example, in attempting to make his own contribution to the Middle East Process, he started workshops encompassing Israelis, Palestinians and Jews. His working hypothesis is that the Jews have an internalized ghetto and the Palestinians have a mental prison. Internalized ghetto and mental prison are both different but closed concepts; the first is a closed community, involving young and old, men and women, all working within the boundaries of their community. The prison on the other hand is a partial, totalitarian, simplistic institution, not ever mixing up men, women, and children, and there are few opportunities for exchanges other than homosexuality or cigarettes. The prison is also limited by time, which changes according to the penalties imposed. This explains why it is much more difficult to get out of a ghetto than to leave prison. He poignantly adds: "The fundamental objective for the Palestinians is to prevent them moving from prison to a ghetto. The second objective is for the Israelis to leave the ghetto without moving into a prison." For him it is necessary to work out a process of internalization of peace in which one side has to come out of its mental ghetto and the other out of its mental prison.

He goes further in elaborating, "the only way to ensure that the Wailing Wall doesn't occupy all of our life, is to build the wall of Interpretations. To prevent the Wailing Wall from becoming an obstacle, a prison, one must contribute to the erection of the wall of Interpretations, because interpretation carries freedom, a freedom that is of course relative, and conditioned. Life itself can be understood as a zigzagging between the Wailing Wall and the wall of Interpretations, which is as relevant to the life of an individual as it is to the life of an institution."

Although I was not part of the Israeli–Palestinian workshops I was fortunate enough, much later on, in 1987, to be invited to be part of his staff at the first International Caribbean Conference in Tobago. Here I saw him as a real pioneer and became aware of his immense resilience and his search for truth. He is driven by his own convictions, I had first hand experience of this the first time we went to the Caribbean to originate and commence his work on Leadership, Encounters and Transformation. He strongly believed he could, with the help of his team, make profound changes in the Caribbean people used to European colonization and who justifiably, due to old experiences, initially considered the whole enterprise with much suspicion and disbelief.

He took it on with such a driven attitude that it created a lot of conflict with the rest of the team. At first I was surprised and angry at what I thought was rather cruel, and unnecessary, fastidiousness and search for perfection. Only later on, and again in reflection, was I able to comprehend that this was the only way a leader could function in such inauspicious surroundings. Although he is the first to enunciate clearly the need for consultants to work together with their colleagues, he is also only too painfully aware of the loneliness of the position of Director of the Conference. Decisions have eventually to be taken with the input of the ideas and opinions of all staff, but the final responsibility belongs entirely to the Director who has to be prepared from the very start to be extremely unpopular. At times he is hell to work with, but we all wonder what makes us want to do it again and again. The answer is very simple, we learn a lot. And the outcome? It is that after six years of consistent hard work, the Caribbean is in the process of transformation and has secured a better-defined structure, making a serious impact in many important organizations.

The coexistence of mythical and historical times became strongly apparent in one of the Caribbean conferences, of which I have written elsewhere. I will also give some background information to explain better the complexities of the example.

Transformation is particularly relevant in the Caribbean. The Caribbean is characterized by diversity, the most important is the diversity on its human basis. The natives were treated as trading objects, taken away from their own lands, and transported in the seventeenth and eighteenth centuries by ship to the Western world where they could be sold for the purpose of cheap labour. Since then time has moved on, but have memories of these painful experiences also disappeared? Or have these memories become the significant traumatic experiences, which, despite the transition of time and passing of generations, have remained within its people, affecting their potential for transformation? Had the original and severe traumas become part of their own cultural and social patrimony?

Leadership, for a long time, was automatically considered to be the monopoly of the ruling classes. Dehumanization of Africans was the rule until they learnt of their own capacities, capabilities, and competence when put to the test with good education, and a determination not to let themselves to be mistreated. They were supported in this quest by the wider knowledge gained of their condition from the world around.

This sort of conference is designed for persons who like to better understand, fulfil and develop their roles in a responsible manner. They may come from industry, education, religious organizations, social services, health care or the public. This particular conference had 26 members and there were 16 men and 10 women, with different gradations of colour from very black to very white. The occupational grouping was from financial services, organizational development, religion, public relations, police service, medical practice, telecommunications, general management and public utilities. They were all sophisticated professionals with high profiles in their own working situations. The staff of the conference mirrored some of the characteristics of the membership with differing professions, colour, religion, nationality and culture being represented.

The event outlined below is an example from the plenary of an Institutional System Event that took place close to the end of the Conference. Institutional System Events are designed to study the nature of the relations between staff and members: the staff for this particular event, being divided into management and consultancy.

At the beginning of the Institutional System Event members were told by David Gutmann, the Director, that for the first time they had the possibility to link with the staff, both in their role as consultant and as management.

The general climate prior to this plenary study system event was very much characterized by dependency, with rebelliousness and a great degree of ambivalence, with the refusal of any process of transformation. It took a strong will to stay with the authentic power of this region, conservative and protectionist. We believe that the reason for this "malaise of being stuck" had to do with the fear of the unknown, suffused with feelings of panic, which automatically stops any attempt to try any process of transformation. There were several pieces of evidence leading us to believe that at that point they felt very much in a "status quo" position about their own development. They did not try any alternatives, they hardly formed any sub-systems, and if they did they never took ownership of them.

Before the last plenary of the ISE was assembled, the management deliberately decided to confront the members with "a situation of organized chaos". Prior to the members coming into the room, the staff placed all the members' chairs in different piles in complete disarray, making it look like a complete mess. In contrast, all chairs belonging to the staff, either management or consultants were organized neatly.

The intention was to offer a provocative and strong challenge created by their own confrontation with such chaos that, we assumed, would shake them out of their own traditional, conservative mind system in which they were completely stuck. We hoped that some innovation and creativity would be the response. Staff members took their own positions a few minutes earlier to avoid the likely, in our own minds, situation of members' taking our own chairs and our own positions.

Little did we know of the surprise we were about to have as we entered the plenary room? We were completely amazed to see that all the chairs had been organized in the most traditional and conservative way. All the chairs had been placed in meticulously spaced even rows, facing the management and the consultants. This organization of chairs was far more conservative than any previous ones. All members were already sitting very still, except for a young black fellow, who was standing on his own, looking out of the window. I knew him pretty well since he was in my transformation study group and I knew him to be a sort of obedient "nice mother's boy" who despite his being rather young had been able to achieve a very high position at work.

The meeting started with all the members sitting down opposite the management, they confronted the management, and complained in a very active and normal way. The most vocal and vociferous complaint had to do with what they saw as a very dictatorial and authoritarian management. They went on to say that the staff had created, through both the management and the consultants, a very brutal system of law and order, almost to a fascistic degree. The complaints were voiced in a rather eloquent way. This was met by a matter of fact, cold intervention by one consultant who just told them how the evidence proved exactly the opposite of what they were complaining about.

The evidence, he went on to say, had to do with the fact that the staff had left all members' chairs in such a messy, disorganized way for them to be able to be innovative and creative in rearranging them in an alternative way of their own choosing. Instead, the challenge had been left uncontested and members had responded with their own state of mind, which demanded a very strict sense of law and order. They had resorted to denying themselves the possibility of taking up the leadership role, and creating a new situation leading to transformation. This clearly demonstrated that they were stuck in safety and conventionality.

Members were very much shaken by this revelation since most of them had assumed that the chair organization had been the result of the staff's actions. They began to ask one another who had been responsible for the reorganization of all their chairs. To my own concern, and some degree of anxiety, the young black fellow admitted he was the one responsible. He explained that he had arrived earlier and on seeing the "awful mess" in the room he had felt the need to make order on behalf of his colleagues, and had done it in a very short period of time. Suddenly his behaviour, which he had assumed to be exemplary and expected to be praised by everyone, had completely changed. Not only had it become reprehensible but also it was completely disapproved of by both his peer group and the staff. There was a complete silence, accompanied by a total stillness. People who earlier on had been physically and verbally very active dared not move.

After a long and still silence, experienced as being filled up with a complete numbness and dullness, there were a few feeble attempts from some members to produce some action. Eventually a few members stood up and talked in a rather uncharacteristic way, timidly and awkwardly, very different from the challenging tones used previously. We were stunned by their speeches which resembled little boys, the "girls" kept quiet showing how good, obedient and what fast learners they could be.

Everything felt barren, stuck and paralyzed.

I'll be grateful forever to our Conference Director, Professor David Gutmann for his unique vision, creativity and insight shown when suddenly he offered us a working hypothesis, using the metaphor of the journey of a cargo boat from Africa to the West for the purpose of slave trade.

He added to our understanding of the situation by letting us know that during that plenary it felt as if the room had acquired the quality of a cargo boat with the hull filled up with people of an undifferentiated human, almost subhuman, mass without distinction between children, men, or women. This, he said, was very reminiscent of a time a number of generations back when their own ancestors were forcibly brought on ships from Africa to the western world for the slave trade. They had been brutally treated and abused by their captors, the "colonizers" whose leadership had a barbaric and sadistic system in their ships towards the black people who were to become slaves. All sorts of chaotic situations had taken place without the remotest possibility of help. On the other hand, if a captive ever made a call for help this was met with more cruelty to the point of maiming or even killing them. They had introjected their ancestors and their enormous suffering after living in the Caribbean for many generations.

Now, how to understand their mumbled and childlike speeches made after the silence? Well, during the journey from Africa to the Caribbean, every time they touched a port, there would be attempts by the ruling class of the ship, to get rid of the most troublesome captives and also to make some money out of selling them. The black slaves were made to parade in the market place, to make themselves look not only healthy, but they also had to impress prospective buyers as being extremely acquiescent and subservient, fast learners and hard workers, with qualities fitting only follower-ship needs. That was the reason for their inability to make themselves appear efficient and competent leaders. In fact, if they were to be seen as capable leaders their own survival was at risk. They experienced, following their own ancestors' awful fate, feelings without much hope for the future. Any sense of transformation or innovation was the equivalent of a death penalty, their only way of survival was the opposite, presenting themselves as extremely passive and without any sense of personal authority.

Hence, the working hypothesis was presented as David Gutmann says: "the world of consultants is the world of working hypotheses, whereas the world of managers is the world of working the hypotheses."

We are the real makers of our lives.

Estela Welldon

ABSTRACT

This book is an experience of life, one that reflects other experiences, individual and collective. It carries the desire to bear witness to how much life is founded on experience, and to how only experience can truly make learning possible.

It is based on two convictions. On the one hand, experience is first and foremost located in the encounter with the Other. This work, therefore, takes the form of a dialogue in which the *inter-locutor*, through its presence and its reflection, gives the opportunity for a fertile relationship. A true encounter, in fact, between David Gutmann and Oscar Iarussi, the resonance of which espouses also the flavour of Southern Italy, at the promising confluence between Orient and Occident, and also between Europe and Africa. The Mediterranean, in summertime, is indeed a privileged place and time for reflection and discernment.

On the other hand, the thinking that is unveiled here is the fruit of concrete experiences. It does not directly cross the paths of theory, but prefers those of a school of life that feeds itself through experiences—personal and professional, individual cases and institutional situations—so as to generate, as an afterthought, and without any *a priori*, a few more conceptual elements.

At the same time it demands without any pretensions, that the text read as a treaty *of savoir vivre* (and not *on savoir vivre*).

Three terms describe our existence and constitute its stake: survival; that of catastrophic circumstances or, on the contrary, the extreme banality of life; hyperlife, an evocative neologism that speaks for itself and translates as a daily and threatening trepidation; and life, to be tasted in the *here-and-now*, in constant transformation from birth to death.

This treaty of *savoir vivre* invites us to reflect and ultimately to allow ourselves to act on the limits of our relative freedom. Is this not more than we had previously imagined? Obstacles sometimes come from objective constraints. But in what circumstances do they in fact betray our internal imprisoning?

The quest for freedom, to which the reader is invited, makes its own way along the journey of Transformation. It comes face to face with obstacles, crosses fords and mountain passes, goes through junctions, and unravels in the form of zigzags.

The book is built on ten chapters around a maieutic work that gives birth to a thinking that is first and foremost practice. It ends with a glossary that gives a definition of the main terms that were used.

David Gutmann (Paris, 1950) is a graduate of the Institute of Political Studies in Paris, with a Masters degree in Public Law and a Doctorate in Political Sciences. His mentors are Maurice Duverger and Pierre Legendre and he has been greatly inspired by Wilfred Bion. His analytical paradigm has been constructed through his psychoanalysis with Janine Chasseguet-Smirgel. He is currently Executive Chairman for Praxis International (Conseillers de Synthese/Advisers in Leadership), a company that he founded with Jacqueline Ternier-David in 1989.

David Gutmann is also Executive Vice-President of the International Forum for Social Innovation and board member of the International Association of Group Psychotherapy. An adviser for numerous leaders and managers of companies and other institutions in France and abroad, he is *maitre de conference* at l'Ecole Nationale d'Administration (ENA) and external professor and director of the programme "Leading Consultation" at the University of Glamorgan (Business School) in the UK. David Gutmann has also been awarded the French equivalent of knighthood (*le chevalier de la Légion d'Honneur*).

During most of the eighties, he took the role of staff member at the Leicester Conference (co-sponsored by the Tavistock Institute of Human Relations and the Tavistock Clinic) and continues to direct international conferences on the themes of Leadership and Institutional Transformation throughout Europe, the Middle East, and the Americas. He is also a professional ski instructor.

Oscar Iarussi (Foggia, 1959) is a journalist in Bari. Editor of the culture–communication–entertainment department of the *Gazetta del Mezzogiorno*, he is also a cinematographic critic, consultant to the Biennale of Venice and author of many anthology essays. He is the author of a piece of research on cultural life in Bari, *che ci facciamo qui?* published by Librairie Laterza in 1998.

Introduction

Oscar Iarussi

T he garden of transformation is a little pine grove. It is cool and shady there on one of August's hottest days in Ostuni, Apulia, in Southern Italy. Passing beyond the barn gate, which leads to the garden, the climate is suddenly transformed, freshened by the high trees and the pleasant breeze wafting in from the Adriatic, the Mediterranean, the Levant, and perhaps even from Ancient Rome, towards the garden's little hilltop. The winds become knowledge, a symbolic language, amongst many others, with which to interpret the world.

Creation is a cripple until it is made whole through interpretation, to paraphrase Flaubert. Mere things are inexpressible, empty, and bewitched by a dark and sometimes terrible spell. The enigma of postmodernity demands more than ever that we exercise atavistic, humble, and democratic interpretation. Only interpretation offers the benevolent gift of the other, enabling the passage from an immutable Chronos, who tyrannizes humankind, to the gentle and interlocutory relative time of human relations. It is a passage from the dark to the clarifying fire. Interpretation may stir up the nostalgia of a bygone, mythical order, of a past Arcadia. Perhaps unconsciously, this nostalgia, this future promise, really does exist. But above all, interpretation lives in the *hic et nunc*: it is what is now that needs interpreting and withers behind a minute particle of the world. This is all in the knowledge that understanding the sense of something is not a matter of confining God knows what great miraculous, liberating meaning. Rather, it is a matter of adding another rock to an endless wall that makes a constructive contribution to anything at all, in its unreachable and horizontal evolution beyond the vertical. This is evidence of transcendence's immanence.

David Gutmann suggests spontaneously that the wall of interpretation is the necessary complement to the Wailing Wall in Jerusalem. And later he says that the *Talmud*, book of interpretation *par excellence*, collection of biblical exegeses, has been enriched over generations. The Jewish people are, after all, the people of philology, of the Midrash and interpreters of texts. Jewish implies "sacred language": this is the authentic origin of their "election" . . . but who is David Gutmann? A Frenchman, a Jew, a professor for the last seven years at the Institut d'Etudes Politiques in Paris, as well as a teacher at the Ecole Nationale Supérieure in Cachan, and senior lecturer at the prestigious Ecole Nationale d'Administration (ENA).

His business card says "advisor in leadership", which doesn't mean much in Italian, but could be translated as "consultant in institutional analysis".

In fact, David Gutmann is a psychoanalyst of institutions, both big and small. He carries out his intervention work in the name of his consultancy business, but also under the umbrella of a non-profit making association. He has written articles for specialist journals in France and abroad that discuss the interventions he has carried out. These appear to have been successful, judging by the admiration expressed by some of his clients and correspondents.

His image is that of a "guru" in the realms of psycho-sociology, human resources, strategy, management, and business consultancy.

David Gutmann hadn't written this book yet—that is what he wanted to do with me, although at first I didn't understand why. I had interviewed him while he was on a business trip in Apulia. When I met him again a few months later, he thanked me for the way I had faithfully reflected his ideas.

It was during this encounter that he invited me to write this book, specifying that it should take the form of a dialogue, even though I told him that by using such a format he would risk not reaching a very large readership in Italy. He replied that he was prepared to take that risk. I don't know whether that was out of narcissism or for some other reason. But anyway, I took the risk as well.

We conceived this book under the pine trees of Ostuni, drinking water and smiling at the thought that tourists passing through the barn could perceive us as a slightly bizarre garden spectacle, like the peacocks, the ancient plants, the stony pathway: "look, and there are those two writers discussing life".

It is remarkable that David Gutmann's arguments defeated my reservations in the first place, as they are so hardened by self-irony. This is a spiritual dowry I possess, but also a limiting factor, a means of perpetual self-sabotage. But in this case I was there to, yes, talk about life, to devise an art of *savoir-vivre*, not just survive. The social significance of this *savoir-vivre* is paradoxically nothing more than a guide to good manners. As if it were really more important not to pick your nose in public than to be capable, on a daily basis and in good conscience, of reclaiming the responsibilities and the projections we pass onto others with such unsettling regularity.

This book questions the mode of existence of the individual and the institution. It expresses doubts, but not ones that are paralysing, like "weak ideas", which dissolve the very act of thinking within a simple decline of reason, and not only within positivism. On the contrary, these are vibrant doubts of interpreta(c)tion, enslaved and dialectic, doubts that go along the journey of transformation.

When David Gutmann distinguishes the *project* from the *journey*, conjugating the former as the *object*, and the latter as the *subject*, we gain a simple and invaluable model with which to filter, understand, and once again interpret day-to-day life on the basis of the resounding end of the "great narratives", the "powerful" ideologies, the projects which bathed in blood the era of the Shoa and the Gulags. And it will be easy to verify that in fact these *projects* are not content to fight their own battles. Fixing *a project onto someone else*, as opposed to making a *journey with the other*, continues to scatter projections that are extremely dangerous to individuals and institutions.

Just like history, the route is not linear, in spite of our Hegelian conception of the superposition of the rational onto the real, which is also the other perspective of the drift defined today as "the end of history". The route is a zigzag, full of progressions and regressions, which alternate and run on from each other. Even the journey made by a new ethic that would no longer place itself at the service of a some kind of totalitarianism, and would be able to accept its own limits and bounds, to recognize its own narcissistic wounds, even that would run in a zigzag.

According the David Gutmann, no saviour is really that. Even the concept of "saviour" is becoming incompatible with the idea of leadership, which belongs rather to the universe of the (pre)vision of events, of intuition based on extensive study of their underlying dynamics, of the generation of the only partisans capable of welcoming the role of leader. The temptations of omnipotence and omniscience, however harsh or subtle these may be, are unmasked: they are harmful, sometimes even fatal to individuals or to a system.

History is "opening up", breathing with the same rhythm as nature, rather than plunging us back into chaos. And David Gutmann quite naturally adopts the principle of the transformation of all things. The truth is *the voyage of transformation itself*, since everything is, in fact, continually transforming, nothing is fixed, apart from the fact that we substitute the pulsating secret of each thing with an enigma to be interpreted.

CHAPTER ONE

The generating leader

*P*rofessor Gutmann, what is your profession?

    I am a consultant in synthesis. This profession was created after the war by Dr Gros.

Can we categorize "synthesis" under leadership?

Let's take two intersecting axes: synthesis is situated on the x axis, leadership on the y axis. Synthesis combines several different elements, like systemic analysis, whilst I work on the leadership axis, according to the dynamics of Reparation and Revelation. In effect, I've moved on from Institutional Analysis to Institutional Transformation.

What is the essential feature of Institutional Transformation?

As its name indicates, it has a dynamic element. It's an original way of working with a client: basically, I take on a group in the same way as a psychoanalyst deals with a patient.

And the objective is the revelation of the group's dynamics or those of the institution?

There can be no revelation if there is no transformation. An analysis is, in truth, a transformation. I'll explain what I mean: the explicit objective, even in psychoanalysis, is not transformation for its own sake. What is important is the voyage, the passage. It is like a patient establishing the objective of the change process; that would constitute a block.

Does that also apply to society?

Without a doubt. Let's take Italy, for example. I believe that the social regression in this country, which emerged through Silvio Berlusconi's victory, was a determining factor in the accession of Romano Prodi's government.

Why do you think of Berlusconi as a regression?

With him, the head of the society of the spectacle, of the television, became the head of Italy. But as I said, this regression was necessary. The same dynamic is being born out today in the Middle East. Prime Minister Benjamin Netanyahu represents a very strong regression: the destruction and deconstruction of the peace process, brought forth by the disappearance of Rabin. I have become a lot less pessimistic since I worked on a mixed seminar of Israelis and Palestinians in Jerusalem. For these two peoples, the peace process is inevitable. Before, with Arafat, Peres, and Assad, fear of the awareness and of the advent of something new were predominant. Today, in this new era, the necessity for peaceful coexistence is an established concept.

In the Middle East, however, peace seems to be under constant threat.

To me, the main problem the Israelis have is their mental ghetto, a psychic ghetto, not a psychological one. The feeling of living permanently in a ghetto, which is a very old feeling, but one which was reinforced by the Second World War and by the state of being surrounded, which Israel experienced after 1948. The Palestinians have a different kind of concept: the mental prison. The Palestinian people always carry within themselves a sense of imprisonment within physical walls, and also mental ones.

So basically, we are talking about two peoples, each a prisoner on their own side?

That's it. Rabin and Peres on the Israeli side and Arafat on the Palestinian side are striving to unite these two peoples. Political resistance towards this will is absolutely understandable. Nevertheless mental resistance has to be worked on, since one side has to come out of its mental ghetto and the other out of its mental prison.

That's a new way of approaching the Middle East question. In Italy we have some excellent commentators on current developments in Israel, but they are often Jewish and are therefore probably themselves unconsciously prisoners of the "mental ghetto".

A pause is needed in the Middle East peace process, in the form of a political regression—this is quite essential from a mental point of view. I'll give you an example. Peres said to the Palestinians and the Syrians: "the territories for peace". On the other hand Netanyahu says: "Peace for peace". And it's Netanyahu who's right! Peace is above all a mental concept. So Netanyahu's victory in the elections represents a regression in the political plan, but this regression will allow for progression later on.

[Time stretches ...]

The time for the internalization of peace has to be privileged. The ghetto and the prison are two very close concepts. To live in a ghetto is to live in a closed community. However, all the community's activities are sustained through its young and its old, its men and its women, it producers and its consumers. This is a universal and whole society, but it is stationary, closed, with only a small degree of highly codified exchange with the outside.

Now let's think about the prison: it is a partial, totalitarian, simplistic institution, as Michel Foucault wrote with extraordinary energy in *Surveiller et Punir*. There is one prison for men, one for women, and another for minors. Within a prison, very little exchange goes on exclusively within its own confines. In the ghetto, a culture is established, sexual relationships are possible, art is produced and businesses are set up; in prison, exchange is limited to cigarettes and homosexuality. The historic consciousness of the ghetto is far older than that of the prison. In addition, the ghetto is a concept which can be applied to an entire people, while prison is a concept that is limited by time and reserved for particular individuals: one goes to prison for a certain period of time, the only exception being for those who are sentenced to life imprisonment. That is why it is harder to get out of a ghetto than to leave prison. The fundamental objective for the Palestinians is to prevent them moving from prison to a ghetto. The second objective is for the Israelis to leave the ghetto without moving into a prison.

Is there anyone who has succeeded in freeing themselves from a "mental prison" or a "mental ghetto"?

President Nelson Mandela left prison after twenty-seven years of incarceration and is now in the process of leading South Africa in a process of liberation, freedom, and democracy. Personally, I consider Mandela to be one of the greatest statesmen of the century because of his ability to have not remained a prisoner in his mental prison after his incarceration. It is obvious today that Mandela's objective is to lead the whites and the blacks out of their respective ghettos.

Would you say that Yasser Arafat could succeed in rivalling Mandela?

Arafat is faced with a lot of difficulties. Politically his leadership is recognized, but mentally he is not legitimate: he is a Palestinian from the outside, who no longer lives in Palestine. It is important to know that power in Palestine is to a great extent the prerogative of the large aristocratic families. I worked for a time at the Arab university in Jerusalem, Al Quds, on the invitation of the president, Saari Nussebeh, with the support of a large public enterprise in France, Electricité de France, within the context of a UN programme. It was clear to me that, despite being Jewish, no Palestinian would ever turn on me, as I was an invited guest of Nussebeh, a descendant of the Palestinian aristocracy, whose power is legitimized by the fact that he is a Palestinian on the inside, who lives in Palestine.

And as far as the Israelis are concerned, where does the path to leaving their "mental ghetto" begin? Has the assassination of Rabin by a Jew hindered this?

Y. Rabin had the ability to lead the Israelis out of the "mental ghetto". He was a Sabra, the name of the cactus fruit, used by Israelis born in Israel to define themselves. In addition, Rabin had won the six-day war and he inspired confidence. Even his name, Rabin, was a guarantee for his people. On the other hand Shimon Peres, Rabin's ally, is a very intelligent man with a great strategic vision, but he is a Jew from the ghettos of Eastern Europe. The Rabin–Peres partnership was truly extraordinary. If it was Rabin who was killed it was because, even without Peres, he could have won the elections, but not the other way around. Rabin's death, as absurd as it may seem, has restored a positive normality to the Israelis. It was a death at the hand of a Jew. It's terrible to say this, but the fact is that the assassination of Rabin was a very regressive event that nevertheless facilitates progression. Now we're faced with a taboo: no one really talks about it in Israel.

Could we conceive a hypothesis by which institutions are established through a trauma? After all, Rome was born of a fratricide, and every civilization is founded on a tragic myth, often a violent death.

It's possible that Rabin's death could be the founding act for a new Israel. Just as it's possible that, in order to gain a new Palestinian state, we will have to wait for the death of Arafat: but bear in mind, with regard to this murder hypothesis, I don't believe that he will be killed at the hands of an Israeli. It's more likely to be a Palestinian.

In Italy, the founding act for a new society can be associated with the assassination of Aldo Moro, the leader of the Christian Democrats, killed by the Red Brigades in 1978. This was a genuine "sacrifice", desired by almost all the political parties of the time, who refused to negotiate with terrorists for reasons of State. The sacrifice has never been recognized as such, but that's what it was for Aldo Moro, if one looked at the letters that he sent to his family and to his party's leaders and other groups.

I agree. Moro, just like Rabin, was an innovator who came to be sacrificed. Transformation inevitably undergoes sacrifice or mourning.

More to the point, I would even say that mourning, as the transformation of guilt, is one of the lessons of transformation. Even De Gaulle sacrificed himself in the 1969 referendum, which coincides with the creation of contemporary France, leading to the dawn of the Mitterrand era eleven years later.

I still haven't asked you how you "discovered" the concept of "transformation".

There is a link to Italy. In 1990 I was invited to Milan by ISMO, a training and consultancy institute, which is the Italian equivalent of the International Forum for Social Innovation. The subject of the seminar was training. I was supposed to leave on an Alitalia flight from Paris, but because of a strike the aeroplane hadn't arrived at Charles de Gaulle airport. It was late and I was forced to go home for the night, with the intention of eventually leaving very early the next morning with the first Air France flight. It was then that I started to forge the concept that training[1] is really a Transformation. This was a significant time in my life. My father died in 1987; I completed my own analysis, which had taken seven years, in 1988. In 1989 I left my former company to found Praxis International and in 1990 I was asked to come and teach at the "Institut d'Etudes Politiques", "Sciences Po" as it's called in Paris.

As you mentioned the death of your father, perhaps you could tell us a little about your family?

My parents are Polish, from Lodz and Kazimiecz, although my family probably originates in the Alsace, from where a lot of Jews have migrated to Poland over the past centuries. My father lost all of his first family, his wife and three children, during the Shoa. He managed to save himself by hiding. My mother was born in 1922 and was also in the Nazi concentration camps, Auschwitz amongst others. All this is far from being expiated, because until the age of thirty-one I never knew about my family's history. I began my analysis in September 1981. In February 1982 I went to Israel with my wife, Annie, to meet survivors who had known my father. And there I encountered an old teacher called Sonia. She had conceived and produced a book of several chapters, each of which had been written by one of the old surviving residents of Kazimiecz. One of these chapters was by my father.

And you had never had a notion about your father's past? How is that possible?

My father didn't talk about it, in order to protect us. In fact this did us a lot of harm. I have an older sister and a younger brother: the three of us children came in exactly the same order as those my father had with his first wife, the family killed during the war. My whole life has been dominated by life and death: I would not have been born if it hadn't been for the death of the first family. You asked me if I ever suspected anything. Unconsciously I knew something, I guessed, otherwise I would never have hurt myself so much. At the age of ten, I was crazy; I used to do things like walking on rooftops … And my brother, at a certain point in his life, practically sacrificed himself for the sake of having the past revealed. My father never mourned his first family, and this absence of mourning has remained. It is not by chance that our family was obsessed with the need to care and to cure. My sister is a pharmacist, my brother a cardiologist, and as for me, at the age of thirty, with a political sciences diploma under my belt, my father offered me an income to start medical studies …

A lot of Jews favour medicine. This is clear if you look through the Nobel Prize yearbook.

That's true. For a Jew there are three favourite professional choices: medicine, which of course maintains a link to death and suffering, because, as an old Jew once said: "it's better to be the doctor than the patient"; law, because "it's better to be a lawyer than to be in prison"; and music. For this last one there isn't a proverb, but music is also associated with the transformation of suffering. Do you know this Jewish riddle: "What is the difference between a shopkeeper and psychoanalyst? One generation!" After the Shoa, Jews "could" only choose professions which were extremely mobile, which permitted escape, exile: hence psychoanalysis, medicine, law, and music.

Let's go back to the mourning that your father didn't go through.

Mourning is the archetype of transformation, the matrix of transformation, for individuals as well as for a community. It's rather strange that in my lifetime I had never mourned until my father died. I had had no previous experience of bereavement, since I didn't have any grandparents or uncles: they all died during the war. It's good to have lost your grandparents first, it's a kind of lesson in mourning ...

We talked about the trauma that often forms the origin of an institutional transformation, and we bore out this hypothesis in certain historico-political situations. But are these dynamics also applicable to companies? Could you give us some examples?

SNCF—the French national railway company—was created in 1937. In May 1994, the government appointed a new SNCF chairman, who embarked on a renewed policy aimed at transforming the enterprise. The chairman called upon me straight away to be his advisor and I started work in June 1994. During the months of September and October 1995, Juppé's government, with the support of President Chirac, carried out three measures, which caused quite a commotion. Two of these were a reform of the Social Security system, in force since 1947, and a new definition for special pension schemes, including that of the SNCF. The third measure was the renewal of the contract between the SNCF and the government. This provoked a strike, which literally blocked France from November to December 1995. For its part, Juppé's government chose to use the chairman of the SNCF as a scapegoat, and he was "resigned". This is a good example of a trauma that is contrary to the concept of the founding trauma. To carry on the story: the government chose a new chairman for the SNCF, who asked me to continue my work together with him, even though I was still to go on advising the former chairman during this difficult period. Six months later the new SNCF chairman was placed in custody and accused of corruption prior to his current post. The railways now have a new chairman, the third to be appointed in two years. (If this one asks me to work with him, I'll refuse. Why? Because French Society has decided to blow up the SNCF, rather than to transform it.)

Your vision is rather pessimistic. Why is that? Is it because this intervention fell through, or for another more extreme reason?

The SNCF has become the symbol of a France of the past. It has 180,000 employees, which is a huge number. It is overly bureaucratized, yet on one hand it retains its saintly image because of its past resistance to the Nazi invasion. On the other hand, it remains society's symbol of the first industrial revolution. So, when it is no longer possible to transform the past and to mourn for it, transformation becomes impossible.

There are two kinds of trauma: the first is a founding, creative, generating trauma; the other is a destructive, sterile, mortifying trauma. Elsewhere, despite corruption, the railways are in the process of transformation: this is the case in Germany, in England, and even in Italy. When the first chairman asked me to join him, I basically told him two things. I pointed out, first of all, that the SNCF was undergoing a depression. It had failed to mourn: there is really one type of depression which comes as a result of mourning, and another which is due to the absence of mourning. There is also a "melancholic" depression, when mourning is denied, but that is a psychiatric illness, which is practically impossible to cure. The second thing I talked to the SNCF chairman about was the socio–technical approach employed by the Tavistock Institute: knowing the means by which technique affects social issues. For example, it would be interesting for you as a journalist to know more about the way in which the technique used to design a newspaper influences the culture of those who write it, journalists first of all. But let's be clear, I'm talking about the Tavistock approach here, and not the "Davidstock" approach, i.e. mine . . . (that was just meant as a joke!) So I told the chairman: "You are like an engine driver who derails because the railways have a symbolic value to you, in the fact that you are following rails built by someone else.

What is this symbolic value?

Railways are like telephones: they are umbilical cords. Do you know which country in the world has the greatest per capita distribution of mobile telephones?

I don't know. Italy, I suppose . . .

Italy is nearly at the top—it's in second place, because telephones allow Italians not to cut the cord which connects them to *la Mamma*: this idea was even taken up by advertisers in one of the first commercials for Telecom Italia cellular phones. But Israel is in first place: it's astounding to see, for example, Israeli soldiers with telephones on their belts, next to their sub-machine guns. Who knows, maybe one day we'll see military orders that say "the use of mobile telephones for conversations with mothers is strictly forbidden during service operations!" This regulation has already been implemented ...

Coming back to the railways, your comment about the "derailment" of the chairman who was seeking transformation, was this a "revelation"?

I try to reveal the *hic et nunc*. My concept of *revelation* does not only include what is known as psychoanalytical *insight*, there is also an element of *input*, which can lead to an *output*. Revealing in order to transform. And an insight is not enough: what needs to be added is the shock of great violence that is the output. My work consists firstly of understanding a system in the most complete way possible, in order to then make revelations to transform the system. Incidentally, my company is called "Praxis", which means thinking in order to act. The rhythm to follow could be described like this: reflection, discernment, and action. It was the Jesuits who taught me that. In his *Exercises* Ignatius de Loyola anticipates a first and a second week of discernment. I once asked Father Léon Burdin, chaplain of the IGR in Villejuif (the first European centre for combating cancer), what exactly was meant by "discernment". He replied: "discernment is the recognition and pursuit of ones own desires". My work consists of lifting the veil of desire, of revealing.

Isn't there a risk that your work could be understood as or implied to be a rescue operation, an intervention by someone, in this particular case a consultant, who will set everything up and will succeed in saving the system from its contradictions and its faults?

All processes of rescue, if not salvation, are doomed to failure from the outset. If there is one thing that should be refused, it is the role of rescuer. Because by taking on a role like that one inevitably enters a vicious circle: a person who enters as *rescuer*, becomes a *persecutor* and leaves as a *victim*.

*Rescuer–persecutor–victim: is that Karpmann's dramatic triangle? A
zone at the centre of the triangle which doesn't vouch for normal relationships, which even shows unhealthy relationships between individuals.*

The principal danger arises from the temptation of either
omnipotence or omniscience. These are twin concepts: on the side
of omnipotence we find dictators, megalomaniacs, gurus; on the
side of omniscience the most obvious types are philosophers and
managers. Omnipotence corresponds to the myth of Atlas,
omniscience to the myth of Prometheus. On the other hand, we
need to be able to accept that we don't and we can't know
everything: there is something which I call a *black box*, a box in
which things remain invisible to our consciousness. If we try to
open this *black box*, in other words, to know everything, it becomes
Pandora's box, from which all sorts of ills emerge, above all, a
totalitarian way of thinking.

*What do you do if, despite what you have said, you realize that
someone is continuing to perceive you as a "rescuer"?*

If unconscious forces are at work that really hinder transformation, it would be better in all cases and not just in this one, to give it
up—this includes my own personal safety. Because the sacrifice I
make, or that made by those who work with me, would certainly be
useless. If, in the situation I described, the new chairman of the
SNCF were to end up wearing a saviour's halo, he'd be finished, he
will have signed his own death warrant. And what's more, it's
likely that if he wants to last it out, paradoxically he will have to do
nothing significant in the sense of transformation: if he does
anything significant he'll be finished.

How can you be so sure about that?

It's not a matter of being sure, it's a working hypothesis.

*It's strange when you said "working hypothesis" I thought for a
moment you were talking about the work, the labour of giving birth.*

I love those linguistic ambiguities, because they pick up on signals: my role, in effect, is a maieutic role, a bit like that of a midwife. We should remember that *revelation* is not a lone task, but one that is *shared*. True management is *shared*. That is also the case in any authentic revelation like that, for example, which occurs between an analyst and a patient. There is no true revelation without dialectics. One day I was talking to the technical director of the French railways and all of sudden he said to me: "You know, I feel like I'm at the bottom of a well." It's hard to think of a better definition of depression—this and that of the institution at the centre of which he was working—depressions which are intimately interwoven.

Should leadership, even in terms of the political sphere, be shared? Isn't that a bit difficult to conceive?

It's not exactly like that in politics. A leader is someone who has a vision of the future before others, who has a brainwave, an insight.

"He who limits himself to anticipating his own era deserves to be followed". Ludwig Wittgenstein wrote that in 1930, and the philosopher Massimo Cacciari, who is currently mayor of Venice and one of the unelected leaders of the Italian left, has made it the leitmotiv of one of his books.

I don't know that saying by Wittgenstein, but I agree. But I would add that a leader is not really one if he does not possess the ability to have disciples, to promote his succession. Authentic *Leadership* is generative and generous about the future.

How do you distinguish a true leader from a false one, for example, from the head of sect, at a time when "ascetics" of all kinds are bursting out into an unknown territory brought forth by the anxieties of the end of a century, and proselytizing?

We can cite three differences. Firstly, a leader strives for life, freedom, what we call *radiance*, emergence, whilst the head of a sect is orientated towards death, *domination*, or towards ascendancy, influence over others, and also the appropriation of other people's lives. The second difference lies in antinomy: authority versus power, leadership versus sectarianism. As for the third difference, this lies in a leadership quality which we have already mentioned: a leader is a progenitor of ideas, actions, and successors, be they within his circle of influence, by his side, behind him or even against him. A leader is a generator—generative and generous.

Your answer makes me think of two things, one written by an Italian author and the other by a French historian. The former was Pier Paolo Pasolini who asserted in one of his "scritti corsari" in the Corriere della Sera: *"I have no influences, other than those which derive from my authority." In saying that, he was distinguishing knowledge from power in an era when the two were tending to coincide. The latter is the historian Marc Bloch, who, among other things, taught us to think of history not as a succession of great events, like a military or economic history, but like a succession of generations. And generations are linked to genesis.*

I regard Pasolini as someone with a very broad-scale personality, and I think the distinction which he established between influence and authority is quite enlightening. As for the rest, a true leader is, without a doubt, a generator. A good manager endeavours to build, to exercise, and to share the vision of a leader. A manager can also be a leader, but not always.

Now I'd like to briefly return to *the working hypotheses*. I don't believe that a hypothesis can concur with *the* truth, because there is no one single way of seeing things. If you and I stop for a moment to look at that palm tree in this garden where we're working, each of us will describe the palm tree in a different way. In fact, the palm tree is not only what you say it is, but also what I say it is, and all the other things that we miss out in our descriptions. That is another aspect that differentiates a leader from the head of sect: the possibility of interpretation, which, in the context of leadership, is never unequivocal. For the last three years I have been studying the *Talmud*, with the aid of a rabbi's book. And through reading the *Talmud* I "discovered" that the Jewish religion is the religion of interpretation. The *Talmud* in fact says: "Every man is where he is in order to add another stone to the wall of interpretation". That was how I realized that my culture is impregnated with the *Talmud*, with biblical exegesis, in which the new interpretation does not replace the previous one, but rather adds to it. This is a message of tolerance, of the multiplication of interpretations. In the *Talmud* we can also trace the process of the construction of mourning: we accept the idea that one's own predecessors, however great they were, died in order to form new space for creation. Unfortunately, there are certain religious Jews in existence today who forget the essence of Judaism itself, which coincides, in this sense, with dialectics. Moreover, the very fashion in which you and I are writing this book together re-imposes the way I practice my work, which is always something that is shared with others, subject to the dialectics of interpretation.

Might there perhaps be an unconscious "prohibition" within you about writing a book alone? I'm thinking of what you told me on the subject of the survivors' book, collated by that teacher in Israel, which included a chapter by your father. A "secret", collective book that could have planted "seeds of prohibition" in your family, forbidding you from writing a book alone.

What you're saying is possibly true, but the fact is that I need other people. We simply can't live if we don't accept others. Given my perpetual encouragement of the necessity for dialogue, to write this book alone would have been an ontological contradiction. In that at least there is no parental prohibition involved.

If we wanted to construct this "necessity for others", how would you summarize the concept?

In a phrase with a Galilean consonance: "When you become aware of something, think about all the other things that have already been discovered." The qualities of a leader are not the only thing to be taken into account; consider also, among other things, those of the successor. Being a successor means having the ability to make something new understood and/or to bring something new into action. Personally, I don't ever want to have followers who repeat my teaching or my path. What I would rather see is my successors creating their own concepts. You know, each of my three sons has four names, reconstructing the family which disappeared, because I didn't know my grandparents, my uncles, my aunts, my cousins—they all perished in the Shoa. My eldest son is called Michael-Dan-*Aaron*-Désiré; the second one is called Rafael-Elie-*Moise*-Bienvenue, and the youngest is Benjamin-Gabriel-*Josue*-Aimé. The third name of each son summons up the history of the Exodus. Aaron was Moses' interpreter. When God spoke to Moses, he repeated God's words to Aaron, who interpreted them for the benefit of the Hebrews. Moses therefore needs Aaron. God's words, not always, but often, need two interpreters. The Bible tells both of the *revelation* God gives to the Jews, through Moses and Aaron, and of the *action* ... Moses, together with Aaron, led the Hebrews towards the Promised Land. But Moses wasn't able to enter the Promised Land, as he died shortly before reaching it. He saw it from afar and then died. And so the one who actually led the Jews into the Promised Land was Joshua, who then divided it up amongst the tribes of Israel. It was only after Joshua that the tribes became a nation. I think this is a fantastic metaphor, not only for the ontological impossibility of omniscience and omnipotence, but also for the genesis. It was because God needed Moses to speak to the Jews that he chose him; but Moses needed Aaron to speak to the people, and he needed Joshua so the Hebrews could enter the Promised Land. And when the Jews were worshipping the Golden Calf, Aaron appeased Moses and Moses appeased God. This is the metaphor that I wanted to bequeath to my sons: each of the three of them has their own role and each needs the other two.

*   *   *

"It is not a coincidence".

This phrase by David Gutmann is to become customary during our time in Ostuni. It is August 13th and, at least according to Le Monde, *it is hotter in Paris than in Apulia. David studies the newspaper's headlines and lead columns like the entrails of a vaticination, which, out there in the garden where we're working, confirms and commends our discussion. Even the weather is no coincidence but is rather a symptom of the complexity, the unpredictable character of things. The cool air will make it easier for us to work.*

During those few days, Le Monde *was initiating a big debate about the concept of progress, and in the morning, during the half hour preceding the "official" start of our dialogue, we read the discussions on this subject. It's me who brings David the newspaper. I buy it in Ostuni when I'm crossing town by car to go to the barn where David is staying and where we work: my hotel is actually directly on the opposite side of the "white city". We are separated by seven kilometres, part of which distance is composed of the most inconceivably complex ring road traffic, with pointless roundabouts in the middle of empty, squalid suburbs that scar the landscape. Of course there are no signposts, as if to symbolize the circle of chaos in southern Italy where, for years, public works have been more "works" than "public", in a social, mafia kind of way. But at a certain point the route starts to descend down the amazing Ostuni hillside, towards the plain and the sea, which I catch sight of on the horizon like a close and unreachable mirage. David is, in fact, really here on holiday with his family, his wife, Annie, and his three children, but really his only intention, I would even say desire, is to work with me. My swimming trunks are going to stay in my suitcase, far from the hotel pool.*

From the very first day the road makes me shudder a little. It's a peaceful road, but particularly on the way back, driving up, it stops my breath, breaking up and quickening my breathing, making me grip the steering wheel tight. This is a temporary sense of panic that I don't put down to tiredness brought on by work. And every time I set off back to the hotel, David tells me to drive carefully, as if I'm driving off to God knows what distant destination. When I point this out to him a few days later, telling him about this unpleasant sensation I'm experiencing, he replies that it is no coincidence: during his seminars in Dourdan near Paris, for instance, everyone was encouraged to use public transport, taxis or buses, because a distorted sense of awareness, and thus of the ability to drive, was regarded as a natural occurrence when one is touching the deep core of oneself.

At the same time as buying Le Monde, *I also get some Italian papers, including "my own", which I leaf through first, as usual, but with no lesser feeling of apprehension than that which I usually feel when I'm on leave from work. Forty-eight hours into my holiday, after two months of unremitting and fairly hard editorial work, even though I'm only a few kilometres from Bari, I feel very far away from all that, on a journey during which the time is my own, I'm letting my writing take a back seat, as this is my free time. This isn't a place somewhere outside the real world. On the contrary, the world makes its appearance every morning through the newspaper columns, to remind us that coincidences don't exist. I'm sure that reading the papers every day here in Ostuni with David perhaps* amounts to what Kant called "modern man's secular prayers". The news that catches up with us here in "our" garden—for instance the revolt of the illegal immigrant workers in Paris, barricades in the church of St. Bernard, and a hepatitis epidemic in the Apulian region, which quickly turned out to be less serious than expected—give rise to certain conversations we're having and will have: the other as represented by the immigrant, illness as a metaphor for a system.

On the other hand, it came as a big surprise to David Gutmann to discover that Aldo Moro was originally from Apulia. He knew about the statesman Moro and his tragic end, but he didn't know that he was born in Maglie, in the Salento, just near Ostuni, and that he had started teaching the philosophy of law at the University of Bari, the city that would later elect him into parliament several times. Neither did he know that "my" newspaper was for a long time the daily pro-Moro publication par excellence. Only in the year 1973, when La Gazetta del Mezzogiorno expressed itself in no uncertain terms about its denunciation of the causes of the cholera epidemic raging through Apulia, was an exception made to this support: Moro had shouted at the person who was general manager at the time: "You have reduced my city to the level of a sewer."

The fact that Moro was to make his appearance in our conversation on the day during which we were talking about rails and derailment seems to me to be very meaningful. I tell David about his famous "parallel convergences" between the Communists and Christian Democrats: a formula which was paradoxical, baroque, surreal, as if Moro had dug it out of a verse by the hidalgo Vittorio Bodini, the poet from Salento who was a lover of Spain. According to Moro, the Christian Democrats and the Communists were never destined, thanks to "parallel convergences", to come together, to confront one another, to make the fragile Italian democracy derail. This formula was perceived as a farce, nevertheless it came to make sense, because on the day that the Christian Democrats and the Communists were to meet in parliament, an encounter that was made possible by Moro himself, he was kidnapped and killed by the Red Brigades.

When we were talking about the Railways, I started telling David about my family: about my two grandfathers who were railwaymen and anti-fascists—one of the two of them was actually an engine driver. Family legend has it that he was conscientious enough to be chosen once to drive Benito Mussolini's train, despite the fact that he refused to wear a black shirt. I told him about my uncle who had been a railwayman and my father *who had worked for a brief period on the railways. David Gutmann told me about his family, about his father, his mother, the legacy of the Shoa, about his wife, Annie, whom he met during the unforgettable month of May 1968, and married in 1974, and who would ask him one evening over dinner, with a hint of reproach "why have you been telling Oscar about your family and the Shoa", and he had replied quite simply "because he asked me about them".*

In the three years since I have owned a mobile phone this is only the second or third time that my mother has called me rather than waiting for me to call her—while I'm working with David. "Everything alright?", he asks me when I hang up. Yes, I say, almost strangling myself with my "umbilical cord"!

Everything is alright, but there is a certain feeling of tension within me and around me. It's the first day and at lunchtime I jump into the car with Maritè, the young woman I've come to Ostuni with, to find somewhere good for lunch. A storm is brewing so I suddenly propose a change of plan and suggest going back to the hotel. We argue because, according to Maritè, I'm too focused "on David Gutmann" to realize that she is there and that she's hungry. We end up going to some sort of cellar, which smells bad and is one of those tourist traps, which could urgently do with a visit from the health inspectors. After that day I end up having only a sandwich for lunch, together with David, in the barn. Yet another coincidence?

Note

1.   In French, training is called "formation".

CHAPTER TWO

Living, not surviving

*W**orking hypotheses, interpretation, a level of understanding, and choice: in a nutshell, it seems to me that the route taken in your consultancy interventions lies somewhere between chance and necessity.*

Yes. Above all it's important to interpret in order to choose. Every choice entails an element of suffering. I'm talking about mental suffering and sometimes physical. And this is where we find the distinguishing factor that is choice, and that signifies abandonment, renunciation. According to Mendès-France *to govern is to choose*. I mean governing one's own life. To understand Transformation is to choose to govern oneself. From this point of view, knowing that there will be regressions relieves the feeling of guilt. Indeed regression, deconstruction and destruction are part of life and have to be accepted. Prior to starting work here together, our own exchanges by fax and all the problems that characterized them represented a regression, which went on to enable a progression. Of course, sometimes regression is so forceful that it's difficult to begin anew afterwards. I am thinking, for example, of the kind of regression that an atomic explosion would be: tragic and irreversible.

Could you give me a definition of "regression"?

Regression is *Thanatos*. It is the prevalence of the forces of death in their alliance with *splitting*, division in the midst of madness. I'm talking about splitting in terms of either personal schizophrenia or extreme social fragmentation. Regression is suffering for the sake of suffering, it is the point at which the principle of reality is no longer of any consequence. If Transformation gives rise to the passage from one state to another, in homeostasis everything remains in the same state, whatever the influence of external factors.

Really you're emphasizing the substantial difference between an open system and a closed system.

Yes. In both cases there are boundaries, but in an open system they allow exchanges between the outside and the inside. So, even within homeostasis, there is clearly something positive. For example, our body temperature is about thirty-seven degrees, whatever the external temperature. How do we ascertain that we are ill? When our temperature rises. If we didn't have this indicator we'd be in a much greater danger.

Could you give us an example of social homeostasis?

The Soviet Union encompassed a system in which regression was dominant. In a system characterized by transformation, we have state A and state B. The closer we move to B in our zigzag route, the more B changes; it becomes a mirage, a desire, and a fantasy. It is a desiring fantasy, the vital force, Eros. But within a closed system, which is dominated by homeostasis, all transactions take place inside state A. The predominant principle—despite impulses stemming from the outside, which actually bring about no real change—is that of regression: thus we have more suffering than is necessary, splitting, an absence of the principle of reality, death.

Absolute regression is the kind that brings about the absolute disappearance of a system. The USSR, Mussolini's Italy, Pétain's France were systems of death. They were systems that brought about their own deaths, in addition to the deaths of others. Regression encompasses confusion and fusion. Let's take the case of the Priebke military tribunal in Rome. He was a war criminal, an SS officer, one of the murderers in the *Fosse Ardeatine*, but he was, in fact, acquitted. Italian society was incensed by this judgment, it protested and reacted quite strongly. The Priebke judgment could be considered an essential regression, a necessary reconciliatory boundary. There's some connection between Italian society's disapproval and the fact that Romano Prodi is in government. In my opinion, Italy is a country in a process of Transformation. The military magistrates' regression was essential for enabling Transformation to be confronted. Since then Priebke has actually been sentenced quite definitively.

What do you understand by the term "confrontation"?

On one side there is confrontation, on the other conflict. In confrontation we anticipate an encounter at a frontier, dialectics, genesis. But a conflict or a clash at a frontier is war, a regression that does not include genesis, as each stage of this regression entails more conflict than confrontation.

Could you give us an example of "confrontation" in politics?

The construction of the European Union is a good example. Europe emerged from two world wars thanks to intervention by the USA, and so its regression never had the opportunity to become definitive. It was mitigated by means of external, extra-European input. Since 1945, Europe has moved out of a phase of fighting and entered one of confrontation. This is a phase which was established conclusively through the Treaty of Rome in 1957, thanks to the work of men such as Adenauer, De Gasperi, Schumann, Monnet: here we're talking about real leaders. Hence today the European Union, whatever else it may be, is a union of solid confrontation.

Are you referring to Maastricht, to European monetary union?

I'm actually thinking of the Olympic medals in Atlanta. In the ranking of countries to have achieved the most medals in the last Olympic Games Germany is in third place (twenty gold medals), France is in fifth place (fifteen gold medals) and Italy is sixth (thirteen gold medals). These are, in fact, the same three countries that basically created the Common Market in Europe (together with Benelux), and that accepted, to a far greater degree than others, that they are in a process of Transformation. Great Britain, on the other hand, is only in 34th place with a single gold medal, a country that was being governed under the ultra-liberal madness of a very *minor* prime minister called ... Major.

That's a great inversion of the Latin proverb "nomen omen": the name is a sign of the thing.

For example, De Gaulle put France, the ancient Gaul, back on an even keel, and he achieved this goal in the manner of a cock.[1] However, a country's motto almost always emphasizes its weak point. Belgium, which is a country divided between two peoples, proudly proclaims "strength in unity"!

Let's go back to the Olympic Games in Atlanta.

Germany, France, and Italy together made Europe into the first continent in the ranking of Olympic medals in Atlanta. These countries achieved forty-eight gold medals between them, which is more than the United States and Canada together, more than Russia (twenty-six gold) and more than Asia, at the hub of which China stood out with sixteen gold medals. As for the two Germanys, traditionally very strong in sporting achievement, they gained far fewer medals after German unification than during the time when they were separate. I regard this as a positive result as well, because the great and real fear in France and Italy is that of a Germany too powerful in Europe. In this sense the medals in Atlanta offer a reassuring indication of the state of the world, which leads us to the following idea: *Transformation is the science of life, but it is not a precise science.* The unification of the two Germanys did not actually result in the addition of the medals of the west to those of the east, rather it had a regulatory effect. So we shouldn't regard as dangerous the periodic mini-regressions by such and such German minister or whoever, who protest against Italy's presence in the European Union: these are regressions which enable just as much progression in the Old Continent's process of Transformation.

And you, Professor Gutmann, do you feel European?

When I made my acceptance speech for my nomination as chevalier in the French Order of Merit, I concluded with this sentence: "Jewish I am, French I feel, European I want to be." By saying this I was asserting that I am not a Zionist, but I am pro-Israel and that's why I "help" that State through my work whenever and however I can.

Through your example of the ranking of Olympic medals we've touched upon the way in which your Transformation-Approach works, or am I mistaken?

Yes, the Transformation-Approach is a new way of under-standing the world, it is not *the* world. It's a new approach, which I believe carries a lot of common sense and which is not fatalistic. On Transformation's zigzag pathway, we need to struggle to increase the "zig" and decrease the "zag". The role shared between the leader and the consultant involves characterizing and discerning when and how a new regression is beginning. Recognizing in order to act and halt regression.

Is this an approach you believe can be applied to other cultures? I'm thinking of Islam.

On the basis of my experience I would tend to say, yes. This was affirmed to me by, amongst others, a young Palestinian woman, who was a practising Muslim, and who participated in one of my seminars in East Jerusalem. She managed to express the journey of Transformation in a very eloquent pencil drawing.

In the Transformation-Approach, and particularly in the alternation between regressions and progressions, are there any useful indicators that enable one to "read" what is happening?

There are the "three Bs". Three mechanisms, three roles, three terms that begin with the letter B. *Buffers* curb progression, but *Boosters* promote progression and *Blockers* stop regression and constitute a resistance mechanism.

What are the origins of these three words?

The term *Buffer* is used in the railway and automotive industries. The origin of the word *Booster* lies in aerospace jargon: it comes from missile technology. And as for the term *Blocker*, this has been borrowed from information technology, and had its baptism of fire during the New York stock market crash in 1987, when Wall Street faced its most resounding and most sudden collapse since Black Thursday in 1929.

Could you tell us in detail how the three Bs function?

Let's start with Buffer, which is actually quite ambivalent: from time to time it can slow down progression, and also regression. For instance, in a business enterprise the bureaucrats—those who I'd call *fanatics* and who others might describe as *reasonable*—are the Buffers. But the most "effective" Buffer is definitely the enterprise's culture itself. Let's now develop a hypothesis, which may appear paradoxical. In my opinion IBM is a dying business, unless it makes up its mind to radically modify its enterprise culture. Its culture remains fundamentally monolithic, one-dimensional, gigantic, whereas information technology is heading exactly towards quite a different culture: it's tending towards the very small. Since we've already used the example, let's refer again to the Atlanta Olympic Games to demonstrate my point. These were disastrous Olympic Games from the point of view of information technology services, which were entrusted solely to IBM. IBM is a multinational company whose structures have changed, but whose culture has not. That IBM commercial where a butterfly appears as if it's a prototype designed on a "personal computer" bears witness to this: we're faced with publicity that is sick with omnipotence. It's as if the advertisement were saying to us: and IBM created the butterfly ... But IBM is not God! So that's what I mean by a Buffer which curbs progression.

You said before that a Buffer can also slow down regression. What did you mean by that?

For example, the people I call *crazy entrepreneurs*, who are the opposite to bureaucrats, sometimes risk leading the company they work for to ruin. It's true that everything that falls under the notion of repetition conceals a positive aspect, preventing what in psychoanalysis is defined as *release*, excess. Transformation also needs this protective mechanism, because it cannot do with totalitarian excess. However, Transformation enables a departure from the initial manuscript, the original *script*, which Eric Berne talks about. The initial script heavily marks individual and collective history. Transformation urges us to leave this track, to leave the Imola racing circuit—always repeating itself, always circular—and to create a new road, one's own journey, the journey of life. The journey is unique for each one of us. Marguerite Yourcenar in *l'Oeuvre en Noir* offers us the most real definition of freedom: not the most beautiful, but the most real. She says something like: *freedom is the freedom to play with the cards we were given at the start*. This also implies the necessity for exchange, exchange with others (beyond "Solitary success!"). And it's clear that we can only play with others if we acknowledge not only the diversity but also the *otherness* of the other, which is the most profound and most radical aspect.

So it's not a matter of absolute, unconditional freedom.

No, it's about limited, relative, conditioned freedom. Because in the end we all die.

What you're saying concords with the "finitude and the beauty of being on earth" that Sigmund Freud wrote on the subject of war and death.

Absolutely. I'm talking about the freedom to refuse totalitarian homeostasis, the freedom to play with others, to *open play*, as one says in card-playing language, to stop playing *solitaire*, to heal of one's own narcissism—by choosing confrontation. This is also what inspired me to formalize my work. I identified, amongst other concepts, with the *social dreaming* of Gordon Lawrence, one of my teachers at the Tavistock Institute of Human Relations in London. It's possible to work on the collective and institutional dimension of a group's dreams. All the more so if one considers that a German psychoanalyst found patients' dreams in his colleague's archives that, at the dawn of the 1930s, envisaged the advent of Nazism and all the dramatic events which ensued.

Is this an example of the collective unconscious that Jung talks about?

No, in this case it's not about Jung's archetypes, but about the *hic et nunc* of patients who were in a situation of apprehension (in both meanings of the word), and who were hence dreaming about something, which then became Nazism.

Can we talk about Boosters now?

Of course. Boosters are all the mechanisms or processes that accelerate or revive the zigs of Transformation, that is, the phases of progression and construction.

So could you give us an example of a Booster in the context of a company?

At the end of the seventies, Honda created a special unit into which it regrouped most of those people, employees, who were creating problems within company culture at the time. Legend has it that in this unit everyone did exactly what they wanted to do. Successive studies have proved that, in the years following its creation, forty per cent of Honda's innovations originated from within this unit. However, in my opinion, a *Mr Innovation*, who would be outside the company's hierarchy, would not be effective to any great degree in the long-term. On the other hand, this policy was an extraordinary accelerator for the factory's Transformation when it reached its peak. This was also the case, for example, during a unique seminar I ran for Intel-Israel's Fab 8 unit, which produces Pentium microprocessors. This is a seminar that we're going to talk about again, and which was characterized by real technology *transfers*— knowledge exchanges in the Transformational sense—from one side to another amongst the company: and this not only because of the training of the consultants, who were chosen within the most senior managers of Intel-Israel itself. These were managers who, their colleagues said rather ironically, had caught the ... "Gutmania".

Is this a moment when, if Transformation has begun, it becomes impossible to stop?

Yes, this is the time when the only way to stop Transformation is to destroy the institution in Transformation. Or perhaps by means of Buffers, which slowly asphyxiate Transformation. And in that case, the seeds of Transformation are then buried in the soil, where they can remain dormant for years before re-sprouting. We also believe that every time there's progression, regression will also occur; otherwise it is not true progression! It's inevitable, because as soon as progression comes about, the elements of resistance to Transformation are mobilized. In other words, I believe that life does not exist beyond its association with death. Death is pre-programmed. The dominant principle of life is entropy, because there is life and there is also death. Only individual or collective beings that have the ability to acknowledge that they will die one day live to the full, in complete awareness.

But being aware of death is also the chief, the strongest source of anxiety.

That's right. It is an anxiety, which, if it doesn't dominate us, if it doesn't become our master, produces creativity. Managing anxiety, which in any case requires a very delicate balance, encompasses either depression or creativity. Fear is fear of something or someone relatively precise, fear of an object. Anguish, on the other hand, is indefinite, indeterminate. Anxiety is something else again that really exists in relation to death. In the face of this dread of death, *we can choose to live or to survive*. Survival is, for example, the experience people had in the Nazi concentration camps: it's a case of heroic survival in extreme conditions, as recounted by Primo Levi or Robert Anselme. But, from another point of view, there is also a banal survival, like in the song by Jacques Brel, which says: "In this family, sir, you don't think, you don't think … you eat". Life, however, is Transformation.

Is there an element of suffering in "banal" survival?

Of course, but only a daily banal suffering, which doesn't go to extremes, and in which the objective of each day is to repeat the previous day. It's a condition that doesn't take into account the passing of time. Time appears frozen, suspended, wiped out. Whilst in extreme survival, the predominant objective is to still be alive in the evening, or the next day: like in the extermination camps, but also in the terminal and irreversible phases of cancer sufferers, at least for some of them.

What does choosing to live mean?

To acknowledge and to accept the passing of time, that is what Transformation is, because the passing of time is a journey from one state to another. Life means to be co-author of this journey of Transformation, to as great a degree as possible. To be a co-author, like in this book that we're writing together, you and I. *Author* comes from the Latin *Auctoritas*, which means to increase and to make something increase, but also respect, credibility, value, and influence. To me, being a co-author means to grow and to make something grow, to become as aware as we can of what is happening, and to do so with others. I can't build the Transformation of my life all alone, the other is co-substantial.

But in a couple or in an institution, the other may not be interested in Transformation. What happens then?

The problem in this case is knowing why we've chosen another who isn't "interested" in Transformation. It's essential to reject the antagonistic outlook *We/Them*—with the *splitting* that this represents—within a couple, a company or between countries. Because an outlook like that is a resistance: when we choose someone who refuses Transformation, it is so that they can carry the projection of *our* refusal to transform. It's a mechanism we encounter partly in Catholic liturgy, when the *mea maxima culpa* is in fact a *felix culpa*. We have to take into account the pride there is in confessing to a mistake in order to unburden oneself of it, by projecting it elsewhere. And so you see, my work consists of making these contradictions emerge, not in order to resolve them, but in order that everyone may experience their own ambivalence.

How do these projections of refusing Transformation work in a company?

What often happens is that in a company the middle management—that is, the intermediate level between top managers and
workers—attract and bear the projections of others, throughout the
company, from top to bottom. Those at the bottom of the company
easily project their own refusal to transform onto the middle
management. The top management will say to the worker: "I want
to satisfy you and improve your work, but I can't because of the
person who is immediately superior to you. It's him who opposes
the improvements and unfortunately there's nothing I can do about
it." And the worker will say to the top manager: "I want to produce
more and better, but the middle management is preventing me from
doing so. He's opposing productivity in the interests of his own
power. It's not the fault of those at the top, but of those on the
intermediate level." Both of them are above all expressing what
they say to themselves and are projecting their refusal to change
onto the middle management . . .

Acknowledging one's own projections and accepting to own up
to them is the sign of an institution in Transformation, an institution
that has chosen to live, not to survive. In fact, a very significant part
of refusing Transformation comes from the tendency that each of us
has to fail to acknowledge our own projections, to the extent that I
would say *Transformation is above all the Transformation of projections*.
My work is devoted to the Transformation of roles, relationships,
systems, and—more recently—projections.

So you are not looking for the Transformation of individuals?

No, my work is not about the Transformation of individuals.
Only psychotherapy and religious conversion can change them.
Some people come to our seminars to find a mystical revelation. I
am against that. My work is concerned with helping people to
understand why someone repeats the same social behaviour every
day. A classic example I can quote is that of a director who attracted
brutality from those around him, while at the same time he was
always brutal towards others. This was *simply* because he had spent
his childhood in a brutal environment and his *script* anticipated for
him the role of *the upholder of justice*.

We're coming back to the concept of the "script", to the childhood scenario, to "distant voices, still lives" to quote the title of Terence Davies' beautiful film.

Yes, but I reiterate, there is an individual *script* and an institutional *script*. We were talking about IBM: IBM's *script* is to *comprehend the world*. That's impossible! If we want to make the world comprehensible, the consequence of that is to *dominate it*. Indeed, to make something comprehensible means wanting to diminish its complexities, which encourages opening the door to totalitarianism. Not accepting complexity means not accepting the other, and heading towards fundamentalism, towards totalitarian thinking, towards the determination to dominate. Transformation, on the other hand, does not only accept complexity, but it sees it as a resource, with all its contradictions, paradoxes and zigzags.

So we could say that democracy is a necessary imperfection: partial knowledge instead of omniscience, a relationship rather than absolute power, mental equilibrium rather than the delirium of omnipotence.

The Transformation-Approach is a lesson in democracy, it's a permanent and unsatisfactory yearning opposed by resistances gathered into a cluster of different elements. The first true resistance resides in the fact that nature's condition is one of degeneration, entropy, and death. To place oneself in the perspective of Transformation does not mean to reject this condition, but to work through it. Every system moves unconsciously towards death and entropy. Our own lives, whatever we are doing with them, will be over in a hundred years time at the very most. Institutions, however, even those undergoing Transformation, have a fantasy of immortality. This concept exists in families, companies, and nations. But when this fantasy starts to become real, the institution is actually preparing to die. It's dangerous to internalize the perenniality of the institution one is part of, which is what happens when fathers pass the power onto their sons, in small or in large companies, or when, like in *Les Mémoires D'Hadrian* by Marguerite Yourcenar, all possible successors are eliminated in order to fulfil the fantasy of staying emperor for ever. On the other hand, in a company, if we want to be a little Lacanian, to lead an *enter*-prise[2] is precisely to live between the beginning and the end, to do the maximum possible between the *hold* of life and the *hold* of death. This is an interior and infinite vision, a multiplication of the *hic* and the *nunc*. To make the best of life between these two *holds* there is Transformation. Healthy systems do not fight death, they fight for life, for the intensity of *what is here and now*, and they fight in this way against anything that is entropy, in other words, the unconscious psychic force of death.

Does being conscious of Transformation ease suffering?

It's possible that one may suffer less, and one will certainly know why one is suffering!

In addition to the condition of nature, what other resistances are there to Transformation?

Another significant source of resistance resides in the fact that Transformation summons up affects. It's clearly not just a mechanism and it's always confronted with a history of humanity. Transformation creates affects and is lived through these affects, like, for example, the refusal of depression. Consequently we have a mainstream in Transformation, a current, a swing of feelings, in which we have to accept short pauses, where regression often occurs.

What do you mean by "pause"?

Take the case of a commando trained for special missions. These men are intended for objective X, for example anti-terrorism, and for that objective alone. Whenever they are not on a mission or in training these men are resting. Or to perhaps give a more common example, let's consider courage and fear. We cannot always be courageous but we have to recognize the fear within ourselves. It's legitimate to feel fear, and that's not all: fear encompasses an element that relieves guilt. It's healthy to feel fear.

What are you afraid of?

In my work I fear that someone will go mad. I'm afraid of the destructive power of regression, which unfolds by creating an expiatory victim, hindering the emergence of certain truths in a working hypothesis. Because I accept fear, I can also summon up courage. In one particular seminar that I directed for the International Forum for Social Innovation, six Palestinians took part—that was an all time first! Each of them would have had to spend a sizeable amount in order to participate in the seminar and to pay their travel expenses, but they received financial assistance, some of which consisted of bursaries from the Forum. The six Palestinians would have ended up paying out less than ten per cent of their total expenses, but they still didn't want to pay that amount. We risked having to cancel the seminar, which was due to be held in East Jerusalem. This would have had symbolic consequences: it would have meant the failure of an initiative lead by me, a Jew. I was afraid, but nevertheless I insisted that the six participants should still pay the sum requested. The real problem was actually the Palestinians' sense of dependence on others, which was perpetuated by this subsidized or free seminar. This dependence had to be "cut", to enable the seminar's work to go ahead, even if this meant the next one in Jerusalem falling through. The closer one gets to a Transformation actually taking place, the more resistance one encounters, and this resistance becomes increasingly fierce. I learnt that through experience. The fact that a Transformation is taking place is really proved by the emergence of resistance. It's a paradox, but that's what happens. Transformation is a passage. As Marie Balmary wrote in Le Sacrifice d'Abraham: "A successful psycho-analysis is an act of passage, and the only way to combat the acting out, in other words the passage to action,[3] is the act of passage!" Passage—and so back to the Blocker, the mechanism that blocks regression—is the best possible Blocker for regression.

What do you mean when you talk about passage?

It's a ford in a river or a mountain pass. The closer we get to this passage, the more it recalls the initial repetitious order of entropy at work.

Is that what Berne described as the "vortex"?

Yes, because order is conservative and reactionary by definition.

Let's not forget that sometimes resistance is the fruit of a consultant's mistakes, but when one is nearing a process of *passage* one needs lots of determination, courage, and faith in order to see it through. Resistances tighten up like a bow, but if one can manage to make the passage, these resistances collapse. The most resounding example of this was the Berlin Wall: who would have thought, even the day before, that it would come down? The same thing can be said about Israel: during the summer of 1993, there was an Israeli raid in Lebanon, followed a few months later by the Oslo accord between Rabin and Arafat, which led to the second fall of the wall of Jericho ...

Passage reminds me of Walter Benjamin's Passages *and of the book's title in Italian translation,* Paris, Nineteenth Century Capital. Passages *as a symbol of modernity.*

It's astonishing that I hadn't thought of that before ... Throughout my childhood I used to walk through a *passage* in Paris to get from home to school and back. I lived at 26, rue d'Enghein, which "passes" across rue du Faubourg Saint-Denis, which in turn begins at Porte Saint-Denis, on the boulevard Saint-Denis. To get to school I had to go through the *Passage des Petites Ecuries*, where one of the national daily newspapers had its print shop. I remember seeing all the great big rolls of paper.

Did you know that amongst the pictures in the Benjamin book, at least in the Einaudi edition, there's a photo of the Porte Saint-Denis taken at the end of the 18th century, which must have been a stone's throw from your house ...

That's really amazing. It's not a coincidence that you're telling me about that and that you're a journalist for another major newspaper too.

So we can now see passage as a symbol of Transformation?

That's exactly my opinion. We could even paraphrase the famous proverb *hic Rhodanus, nunc saltus*. In the *passage* something irreversible occurs, which goes in the direction of Transformation.

*   *   *

The second day begins on the subject of one of my dreams. While I'm driving back up to the barn in my car I don't feel too sure whether to tell David about it or not. But then, once I'm back in the garden, when he asks me casually "did you sleep well?" I find myself recounting the dream to him after all.

> *I dreamt that Annie, David's wife, whom I had basically only met a few hours previously, told me in no uncertain terms that I should get on with my writing. "You have to work", she said to me, "you have to, you just have to, that's what I'm here for".*

David Gutmann takes a while to think about this—not just a moment, or an "attimino" to use the popular Italian barbarism, but a good long time. He takes a puff on his travel pipe, which he's had for years and years, and which he always brings with him when he goes on his trips around the world. He lights the pipe using one of those Swedish matches, which he doesn't throw away but puts back in the matchbox with an almost obsessive sense of tidiness, next to the other unused matches. About five or six days later I decided to ask him about this private habit, and he explained that he uses the matches to relight his cigars, which he normally smokes in the evenings after dinner.

But returning to the dream. I am "afraid" that he is about to offer an interpretation, although that is, of course, also what I desire. One can't fail to see a certain analytical charm in David Gutmann, even if it was basically he himself who decided to "confess" in public. But David doesn't like to volunteer explanations. He simply says that Annie is woman, a mother, and a feminine archetype. "In oneiric language she could perhaps be your mother". He adds, "Besides, you did have a telephone conversation with your mother yesterday on your mobile phone. But the most important thing about this dream is the incitement to write. We're not here alone: both you and I have with us people who love us and who want this book to materialize just as much as we do".

This is true. Each evening from that day on ten-year-old Benjamin, David's youngest son, will ask us how many pages of the book we have written, and whatever amount I or his father tell him, he will reply with a slightly disappointed expression: "I wish you'd done more".

Reading some of David's papers, on the eve of our encounter, they seemed to be cluttered here and there with too many technical words and an overly liberal use of scientific notions, a feature typical of new disciplines that are trying to gain acknowledgement. For instance, I didn't "like" the three Bs of Transformation, they seemed quite dull, and very "American" in their attempt to fit the square peg of anthropology into the round hole of linguistic logic. But when we began to talk in Ostuni things changed. I understand now that even if he is very fond of the idea of academic consensus, David Gutmann is in fact a stranger to the particular type of varsity ritual that frequently, and to an ever greater extent, circumscribes the object of study into ever more restricted, closed circles. These circles usually withdraw around an academic throne, a certain kind of language and its "physiological" colonialism. At the same time any external overtures are presented in papers and at conferences, by means of which they try to win over other neighbouring or distant circles, launching an assault upon them or, at the very least, through an attempt at hybridization. This is a vision of knowledge paralysis, in which the only sense of grandeur resides within making the acquaintance of power: an oasis, a citadel of knowledge, knowledge that is, in the end, phobic.

Not David Gutmann. He doesn't lose sight of the map to these oases, these safest of refuges against the madness that can besiege you in the desert when you have lost all landmarks, and even if you decide to cross it, that desert, that descendant of the Exodus that you are. And he doesn't defy it, he follows it, he strokes its dunes, he listens to its secret heart, he scans its profile. This is natural in David's culture. In that respect, he can sometimes appear to his students or to others to be something of a "shaman". It's the raw and the cooked, to paraphrase Claude Lévi-Strauss.

There is in David Gutmann a coexistence of mythical and historical times, which takes root in his refusal of any project whatsoever. There is no goal towards which to steer history and no saving finalism for one to head towards. It is in this aspect that David is undoubtedly—and I stress the word undoubtedly—least Jewish in his mode of thought: no promised land, neither biblical nor political (the communism advocated by Marx, who was a Jew), nor mental (the psychoanalysis practised by Freud, who was also a Jew). But David's Judaism vibrates quite distinctly at the idea of passage. Gutmann says: "Transformation is to cross a ford", which immediately calls to mind Abraham ha'ivri, "the Jew, the man who crossed the Euphrates". Gutmann says, "passage is the symbol of Transformation." And Passover, the Jewish Easter, signifies passage: it's the celebration of the Exodus from Egypt, of the conquest of freedom.

Stimulated by the notion of the end of the 20th century, this idea of passage is incredibly powerful. It's the renewal of an agreement, and not simply between Jews. It alludes to the campfires lit by nomads on the nights of every (good) sense, obscured by "a crisis of reason". This is a new, but very old kind of humanism, which does not begin with myself the man, but with you the man, you the other, because it is only in your eyes that I can see the reflection of the fires of passage.

Notes

1. "Gallo" in Italian.
2. Enterprise in French literally means between-hold.
3. *Passage a l'acte*, in French, means acting out.

CHAPTER THREE

The journey rather than the project

*P*rofessor David Gutmann, we have talked about the passage of Transformation. You have been inviting us to become explorers who, together with others, interpret the very map of life. *Interpretation is therefore at the heart of your work as a consultant. Let us see what the practice of your hermeneutic is.*

Without being unduly modest or excessively arrogant, to know oneself and to know Life means, in fact, to really be an explorer, as you put it. Every explorer goes a little bit further than the others. And the territories that remain to be discovered are in a far greater quantity than those already discovered. Each new discovery is essential, because it gives rise to more adventure. Thus, each new discovery will be important in itself, *practically*, but also precisely because it prepares the ground for a new one. In that way we are back to the quote from the *Talmud*: "Every human being exists in order to bring another stone to the wall of Interpretations." The wall of Interpretations is different from and complementary to the Wailing Wall. The latter is necessary: indeed, it represents absence—but also memory—loss, destruction, and lack. It is a fundamental symbol of what makes our humanity: imperfection, incompleteness, and absence. But the only way to ensure that the Wailing Wall doesn't occupy all of our life is to build the wall of Interpretations. To prevent the Wailing Wall from becoming an obstacle, a prison, a hold[1] as we say in psychoanalysis, one must contribute to the erection of the wall of Interpretations, because interpretation carries freedom, a freedom that is, of course, relative and conditioned. Life itself can be understood as a zigzagging between the Wailing Wall and the wall of Interpretations, which is as much relevant to the life of an individual as it is to the life of an institution. It is essential, for example, that an industrial and commercial company makes links with its own past and possible failures (symbolically turning towards the Wailing Wall), but also with its own future, with development, therefore switching its sight towards the wall of Interpretation. Judaism, if you think about it, is based on the dialectical relationship between Jeremiah and David, between the prophet of lament and the king who built Jerusalem. A company that loses the memory of its failures is unmistakably sentencing itself to repeat them, and this in a more disastrous and dramatic way. I'm thinking of IBM, of whom we've already talked, or of the amazing banking crisis of the Credit Lyonnais. Some companies sometimes build their own wall of Interpretations; it is the case, I believe, of Fiat, who, in the last ten years, engaged, in a way that only few other companies engaged, in the domain of innovation. Jeremiah and David are both indispensable and complementary: one allows the existence of the other.

Is interpretation always useful? I am referring here to those who advocate that in a period of crisis, or in a case of emergency, one must suspend the dialectic of interpretations and move on to action. In Italy at the start of the eighties, a whole political season unfolded under the name of "decisionismo", a chapter that ended, not by coincidence, with the much publicized inquiry into the "Tangentopoli" corruption.

Interpretation is even more useful in a state of acute crisis. I remember that a few years ago it was the expert use of such an approach that made it possible to avoid heavy human casualties in the hijacking of a Kuwaiti Boeing. It was the patient work of interpretation, on the part of the Algerian negotiators with the hijackers, that moved the situation out of a deadlock without any bloodshed.

Who knows if, by making use of interpretation, it would not have been possible also to save the life of Aldo Moro. At the time we did everything but interpret. The State came across both as very strong and very weak. Some leaders of the socialist party were dealing with mediators who said they were "close" to the Red Brigades, whilst the other political leaders were mainly working hard at exorcizing the terrorist danger, by claiming it was foreign to the sane body of the Italian society. A ballet that ended in tragedy . . .

In the case of the Moro's assassination, I am struck by the fact that interpretation, if indeed there was any, was made *about* the Red Brigades and not *with* them. It is not about convincing someone, but about knowing and self-knowing, and therefore about recognizing.

Moro's assassination somewhat marked the re-emergence, in the political arena, of the Ancient tragic element. Maybe there was no possible solution, the reasons put forward by one side, the State, were not soluble in the reasons put forward by the other side, the Red Brigades. There was a reciprocal irreducibility, both parties "had no words left to contradict each other", to quote Sophocles, and so there was no possible dialectic any more. In that case, does interpretation not run the risk of being an illusory exercise?

The heart of the matter is the difference between convincing and knowing. Military language is inherent to *convincing*: it is viewing existence in terms of war. By contrast, in the notion of *knowing* (*connaitre*), there is the notion of *bringing to life with* (*faire naitre avec*), creating something new that did not exist, a new perception of reality, a possible third life. I am not talking about *synthesis*, but about creating another interpretation. This is true everyday in my work. *Without memory or desire*, this is how—according to W. R. Bion—a psychoanalyst should start every session. In other words, I think of my work as being without the Wailing Wall and without the wall of Interpretations as definite preliminaries. One must dive in and float whilst listening: sometimes swallow a mouthful of water, sometimes float on your back and lie still on the waves. It is an almost ascetic exercise, because *preconception* prevents *conception*, the preconceived is its abortion. The Greek tragedy is still alive and relevant, although in it, more than the *synthesis* of reasons it is their *syntony* that matters. It is not about working with theses and making *syn-theses* with them, but about putting into place the praxis, which is about making use of experiences rather than theses. Experiences are always individualized, they cannot be mixed up, but their encounter can bring about a truly new conception of a part of the world.

An example please, this request is becoming familiar to you?

Mail order, there is my example. Mail order is successful everywhere (except in Italy) because, with that particular market, it is the women who order, in both meanings of the word, *ordering goods* and *keeping things in order* in the household. In that way, they express their power. So I am asking you a question: why is mail ordering less successful in Italy than anywhere else?

I would venture that it is because Italian women don't need mail ordering to express their power within the household.

It is one interpretation. Another could be that Italian women do not exert any power at all within the family, nor therefore through mail ordering. Personally, I agree with your hypothesis. Currently, within the mail order field, the market for clothes has collapsed, and we are witnessing a real boom for financial products, insurance policies, credit, and loans. It is, therefore, a new power that women have conquered, since they are now managing, through this new medium, an increasing part of their household's savings and other financial investment. So, when I started working as a consultant for "les Trois Suisses", one of Europe's largest mail order companies, the first question that I asked myself was to know why its president had chosen that sector. The answer was the following, this domain is, for a man, a way of trying to understand, *but from a distance . . .* the mystery of women, of what a woman is. Over ninety per cent of customers are women. This is what I mean by *creating a working hypothesis*: a hypothesis created with the person who is working and which this person will therefore not be able to refute; at worst he might oppose some kind of resistance. I insist: one creates *with* and not *over* somebody.

I get the sense, knowing also your writings and the headed paper for "Praxis International", which introduces you as a "Synthesis Consultant (Conseiller de Synthese)", that you are now going beyond the notion of "synthesis".

That's absolutely true. I am currently living one of my most recent choices. Synthesis is a result whilst Transformation is a process. The journey is more important than the result. The symbol for strength and wisdom in China is the dragon, because it transforms itself relentlessly. And Taoism is the science-experience of the journey. A famous Zen proverb says that in archery, what's important is not the target but the arrow's trajectory.

Every time someone tells me this Zen story about the bow and the arrow, I think of this song by Francesco De Gregori, which goes: "Dino, don't worry about taking the penalty, it is not on such details that a player is judged. A player, you can recognize him by his courage, his altruism, his imagination …". Courage, altruism and imagination: a little catalogue of end-of-century virtues. Projectable qualities, which do not require a target and wandering virtues, light as the luggage of a traveller who aspires to go far.

The journey is a lot more important than the project. "Cartesian" rationality—even if Descartes was a lot more subtle than Cartesian —has always prioritized the project. The East, however, prioritizes the journey. The great creative mythology is made of journeys: between the Yin and the Yang in China, between the Skies and the Hearth in Greece or with the Vikings, and then the myth's peregrination and in particular the Exodus of the Jews from Egypt to the Promised Land. The way in which a journey has developed is definitely more important than the programmed result, the *a priori* definition of the objective and the project. This resonates with the opposition between Dante and Machiavelli. The Divine Comedy can be read as the story of a travel, a journey. The Prince however, claims that the end justifies the means, it is a project. *To the contrary, it is the means that justify the ends.* One cannot create democracy through imposition, be it with a country or with a company.

What about revolution? Does the violent price paid for injustice and misery justify the means?

The violence always inherent in a revolution does in fact mark its tragic destiny. I am thinking about the French and the Bolshevik revolutions. The word itself, *revolution*, is indeed unconsciously but wonderfully chosen. For *revolution* means a return to the starting point. The Soviet revolution has created a new aristocracy, the *nomenklatura*, an advent that was reproduced with the Chinese revolution. The French revolution did not, in fact, modify the caste system. Furthermore, within a revolution and within the authoritarian regimes that it produces, the usual ambitions of omniscience and omnipotence are not the only ones at work. Omnipresence is also one of them. The fantasy for a man in power is always one of being omnipresent, but in authoritarian power this fantasy is even stronger. This could explain the excessive political iconography in fascism, Nazism, or sometimes communism, but also the interest that dictators have for cinema, or today, in a different way, the invading nature of television. They all represent ways through which power can guarantee a continuous presence. In that context, Transformation is also the acceptance of absence, of void, of *vacuum*. In the Talmudic tradition, itself an exegesis of the biblical tradition, the interpretation of the creation of the world is very interesting: "in the beginning was the void." And it is because there was this void that God wanted and started to create. Void enables creation. Do you remember Bion's phrase, *without memory or desire*. Wilfred Bion was protestant, a Huguenot, but born in India, brought up by an Indian nanny who would tell him her own myths. The *project* is a *projection* matrix: it gives birth to and attracts projections. It is an open door for fantasies at work against reality. The *journey* is an *experience* matrix that enables the facing of reality. Experiences allow on-going learning to occur. Again according to W. Bion and A. K. Rice, the only way to really learn is through/ from experience.

What do you mean by madness in the project?

Madness is the absence of links, of relationships. When someone lives in their own world, he/she is autarkic, and will then project onto others what they can't take upon themselves or accept about themselves. Such is the case of someone who says that "all women are whores", or "I hate homosexuals". A true journey, conversely, can only be made of vicissitudes, of zigzags. The slalom of Transformation happens without post or ski poles! But humans, individually and collectively, are structured in such a way that it is difficult to ask of them that they constantly live in uncertainty. That is why I highly support the existence of projects for a nation or a company: they are landmarks, just like stars or mountain peaks. The real question is not about knowing whether projects are more or less necessary: they are necessary. The real question is our capacity to not be fooled, to not lie to ourselves, to not see that projects are *transitional objects*, to quote M. Klein and D. R. Winnicott.

What is a "transitional object"?

Take the Maastricht criteria, for the European monetary union. The Maastricht treaty is a transitional object, what matters, in fact, is the way through which countries and peoples will get to the single currency. On the other side of the spectrum we have omnipotence, as witnessed with Intel's president Andy Grove, who says: "by the year 2000, there will only be two kinds of processor companies: those who will still exist, and those who will have died." In other words, to follow Grove, Intel will be the only remaining one. We're back to the IBM model, with the ambition for which the science fiction novel *Everyone in Zanzibar* is a satire; in there you can read the following motto for a worldwide company: "what is possible, we can do it straight away, for the impossible, give us a little time." I mean by that that projects are transitional object and as such they are very useful. Conversely, projects are very dangerous if used as definitive objects. The absolute project transforms individuals into objects. The journey, in contrast, requires people-as-subjects. A person becomes object because he/she is bound by a project, whereas the journey requires awareness, responsibility, and partial free will. To undertake a journey, one needs to be a subject. And in a collective, institutional journey, members of the institution need to be subjects, that is to say co-authors of the journey of Transformation. So we are very much back to the difference between a leader and the head of a sect. A leader is accompanied, along the journey of Transformation, by followers, partisans, who nevertheless are active, capable of exercising their own authority. In an absolute project you don't have a leader any more, but a dictator or the head of a sect who also has disciples, but this time they are passive, incapable of exercising their own authority . . .

PROJECT = OBJECT
JOURNEY = SUBJECT

. . . life is always a mixture of that diagram. During the travel of Transformation, everyone designs their own route and at the same time their own way of travelling. The shortest journey between two points is not a straight line, but a trajectory in zigzags, made of regressions and progressions.

How can one unmask an absolute project?

From the use of a possessive pronoun. If someone says: *my* project, they already betray that they are aiming for the absolute. A project is *about, over, on.* A journey is *with.* We continue, for example, to put into place disastrous projects *about* urban peripheries, *suburbs.* Governments undertake projects *about* or *on* certain areas and not *with* those who live in those areas. Because each area is different from the other, these projects always end up badly. The same problem happens with the Palestinians from inside Israel. There are a lot of projects *for* and *about* the Palestinians—very often with their collusion—because they have their roots in a relationship of very strong dependency. The alternative is to allow the Palestinians to find their own journey, and that is what I have, in a modest way, started to do with our conferences: to not bring the word, the new, saviour-like methodology but to create with them a process that enables the construction of their Transformation. For example, as we saw it yesterday, I announced that the director of the Palestinian conference would be, as soon as possible, a Palestinian. Even in big industrial and commercial companies I am tired, for at least four reasons, of big projects. The first one is that big projects often have, as an implicit end, the destruction or the diminishing of trade unions' representation inside the company. The second one is that these projects are linked time after time with drastic cutbacks in the workforce. The third reason is that, most of the time, these projects do not produce any positive effect because they are not grounded in reality. Finally, projects are often tools to

THE JOURNEY RATHER THAN THE PROJECT   49

confirm or comfort traditional hierarchy. The processes in a journey, by contrast, are essential and question the classic hierarchy: they reactivate, in particular, mechanisms for the creation of leaders. We can, therefore, formulate a few pairs of antitheses. A project deals with issues of change, a journey with issues of Transformation. A project is coherent with a Society of show business, exhibitions, of appearances, to quote Baudrillard and Debord; a journey by contrast is *an exhibition of Society*, a true spectacle, the spectacle of tragedy. In a project, individuals are spectators, or at best extras; in a journey they are co-authors or co-actors and most importantly noone is a spectator: a journey is a spectacle in which everyone has their own role. Companies that today have some chances, from an economic point of view—I am deliberately talking about profits—to succeed in the medium term, are those in which the journey is at least as important as the project. And with regards to the individuals, I am not only referring to those who work in the company, but also to those who are their clients. Nike or Coca-Cola, for reasons that are specifically commercial, and not of course out of generosity, give the customer the impression—sometimes true, sometimes false—that it is he/she who constructs and transforms his/her own life.

You talk about a company's "ideology", for as much as it shows itself inside the organization of its work, for example, through communication. A most incredible aspect is that many companies have no awareness of their own ideology: an ignorance betrayed through the technicalities of "marketing" or of a vague appeal for "innovation".

In companies today two tendencies coexist in substance: one founded on the ideology of survival and one based on Transformation. The first tendency can be seen in Andy Grove's omnipotent statements, about which we have already talked a little bit. Grove is, not by chance, a survivor: he survived the 1956 anti-Soviet Hungarian rebellion and his culture is one of survival. Japanese Society, with its extraordinary economic performances, is based on survival. Japan is dominated by immanence given its tectonic position, its frequent earthquakes that leave it in a state of permanent uncertainty triggered by the fear of the final, destructive quake. Gobineau said: "a person is an individual with a project." I prefer, by far, the following saying: "a person is an individual on a journey." A show business Society is a society of individualism, in which narcissism dominates and where, by contrast, solidarity and sharing are forbidden. To the contrary, if a person is unique, the uniqueness of each exists in its relationship with others and it finds its worth only in the transaction with others. A transaction process aspires to obtain an agreement—and not a synthesis—which respects each party's singularity. Conversely, a project produces projections, which themselves can produce projectiles. Projections that are not worked on become, in fact, projectiles, weapons of destruction.

You have an institutional dynamics diagram with a strange name . . .

"*Culbuto*". It's the name of a kids' toy in France.

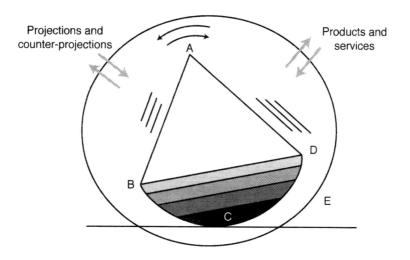

A, structural articulation; B, human basis; C, culture; D, challenge; E, environment.

Let's see how it works.

Most of the time, those who implement change in an organization work on A, on the structural articulation. When the intervention is a bit more sophisticated, B, the human basis, is given some thoughts, which might be labelled "training", or "human resources". In both cases, C, the culture, gets forgotten. But if one doesn't work with the culture as well, you will end up with the *Culbuto* phenomenon: through a series of oscillations, the pendulum's return to its starting point. If the organization is open, E, the environment, will have an effect on D, the challenge, which cannot just be internal, and must be in relation to the environment. In an opposite situation, the organization becomes prey to techno-structure as mentioned by Galbraith, and is therefore at the mercy of the axiom that claims: "the world must be as I say, rather than me being like the world would want me to be." It is the current temptation for all the big corporations, which explains, for example, the worldwide success of Japanese cars compared with American cars. The whole work on challenge, therefore, only has legitimacy with regards to the environment. There is also a time dimension to consider: A is short-term, B medium-term, and C long-term. That is why theories about change only consider A and B, because they need quick results, although these might turn out to be pretty useless. In an ideology of immediate profit and the gain of tangible results, to take C into consideration is not more difficult, but it requires more time.

What does an organization's culture consist of?

Culture is the accumulation of conscious and unconscious phenomena which cut across and construct any organization. The work of a consultant, as much as the manager's work, is to understand what the culture of his/her institution or part of institution is, of the subsystem within which everyone operates. Let's take for example EDF, Electricite de France. EDF produces and distributes *power* within *precarious conditions*. The electricity cannot actually be stored and the electrical system is characterized by a great fragility that relies on the very delicate articulation between production, transport, and distribution. To compensate for this fragility, the culture within EDF is extremely complex and the company tends to exercise an extraordinary power on society. The more fragility there is, the more temptation there is for power. On 19th December 1978, France was subjected to a total blackout. From one incident, the whole of the French electrical system collapsed like dominos, it was as though life stood still. For millions of people, life is determined by electricity: with the developments in information technologies for example, the quality of electric cables' frequency becomes essential in order to not jeopardize the company's data networks. Electricity also has an impact on the landscape—electrical towers, cables, and power stations—but also in terms of regional planning. Electricity requires enormous financial investments, with a long-term design, a nuclear power station for example lasts around forty years.

In that context EDF has become the company of Power, the very essence of the company's power, even though EDF is a public sector company.

Lenin used to say: "communism? It is electricity and soviets." Well, he wasn't mistaken then! Today, EDF's challenge is renewed for two reasons: because it questions its very culture and because it is radically influenced by the evolution in the environment. This new challenge has a double source: Paris and Brussels. Let's talk firstly about Paris. There has been a lot of talk in France about EDF being "a State within the State" or even of the "EDF-State". *Le Monde* (French national newspaper) wrote that EDF's CEO was in fact the French minister for Electricity. It is incomplete: he was the *energy* minister! But this process runs up against a culture in the French State that is dominated by Jacobinism and Colbertism. Usually there is a lot of talk about the former and not the latter, because the latter is a lot deeper and strongly rooted. Jacobinism and centralism were challenged in 1982 by parliamentary decrees initiated by President Mitterand and the Home Secretary G. Deferre, laws which make possible a real and much more important rationalization. However, Colbertism remain untouchable nowadays.

What do we mean exactly by "Colbertism"?

A Colbertist state is a state that doesn't accept that one of its members should become more 'important' than itself so that the State wants to dominate the great national companies. This tendency was inaugurated by Colbert, minister of Industry under Louis XIV, and has undoubtedly amplified right up to the present time. As an example, in the sixties, France was very much behind in the telecommunications field. The general director for Telecommunications (GDT) within the Department of Post and Telegraphs (just like in Italy) was called Gerard Thery. In the seventies, under President Valery Giscard d'Estaing, he launched a modernization program, which met a lot of success. A little bit later, Thery was pushed to resign and the State reorganized the telecom industry. Suppliers, who before were competing, got to share the market between them. On the one hand CGE, the Companie Generale d'Electricite, which was to become Alcatel Alsthom, and on the other Thomson, with help from the State, placed the DGT in check, because the latter was opposing Colbertism. Today Thomson is virtually bankrupt and Alcatel recently lost some forty billion French Francs. Let's get back to EDF. The State wants to punish Electricite de France for its success. Why? It is because France has become autonomous in terms of energy. Electricity prices are amongst the lowest in Europe and because EDF is now the fifth French exporter. In 1996, there were 16 billion French francs worth of sales abroad, including Italy. The quality of the electricity is improving every year; because EDF has at its disposal fifty-five nuclear portions (fifty-eight in 2000) with a high level of safety, because EDF buys foreign companies, and French technology, thanks to EDF, is sold as far as China; because EDF's internal organization is satisfactory (and to be transformed . . .), and its staff of great quality: 120,000 employees, 140,000 if you add Gaz de France; finally because EDF releases a cash flow of nearly 60 billions French francs every year! As paradoxical as it may sound, the State has been punishing EDF and it continues to try to punish it for its success.

How has it been punishing it?

A lot of money is taken indirectly from EDF, by subjecting it to higher taxation than it should be subjected to, by forcing it to take part in the construction of the Rhine–Rhone canal (a project that has now been abandoned), by imposing upon it, before the current one, a president who was merely a politician in disguise, by limiting financially its foreign investments. The French State accentuates its guardianship over EDF, which is the most cost-effective public sector organization, in contrast with SNCF (French Railways) who conversely is the least performing.

By punishing EDF, the State damages social cohesion, technical performance, and economic results.

Let us now get to EDF's second challenge, which we have labelled "Brussels", which in other words means the deregulation of electric energy tariffs in Europe. Currently, EDF holds the monopoly for production, transport, and distribution. European deregulation will make them lose the production monopoly: within a few years from now, a third of the French market will be open to competition. In that context the culture of power and monopoly is facing another challenge: the Brussels-challenge. If a third of the French market goes to competitors, a third of the European market could be going to EDF. It is a wonderful opportunity, which is in keeping with the logic of overproduction, of the quality of the electric system and of EDF's price advantage, unless the State tries to block it, consciously or not, through the relentless Colbertist influence of the French culture.

What was your intervention like, when you worked as a consultant for EDF? What itinerary did you follow?

In my work, I always take, as starting points, affects, or more accurately couples of affects, amongst which "Doubt–Faith" is the most important. The work with EDF happens at all levels, from the basic operators to the board of directors.

Major Affects

GRATITUDE	ENVY
DESIRE	APATHY*
FAITH	DOUBT

*In the French version, the word is atonie, for which there is only the adjective atonic in English to convey its true meaning.

Minor Affects

ENTHUSIASM	DEPRESSION
PATIENCE	IMPATIENCE
PLEASURE	SUFFERING
CERTAINTY	UNCERTAINTY
COURAGE	FEAR
?	?
LOVE	HATE

It involves working with the company's culture (a company that was born in 1946), with the relationship between that culture and the ones in its environment, in particular the several-century-old culture of the French State and, more recently, the European Union's culture. If now I limited myself to make a diagnostic with members of EDF, I would be tempted to say that it is impossible for EDF to meet two partly contradictory challenges: Paris and Brussels. EDF, which furthermore strikes me as the best example of an institution in Transformation, could run the risk of not making it through this new stage. I shall be even clearer: *objectively*, EDF cannot succeed. But there are two reasons that it is fairly likely that *subjectively*, as a *subject*, it will succeed. The first one is that EDF has in itself the experience of Transformation, a *praxis* that it tends to master: even more given that the word *Transformation* is also an electrical term. A transformer converts one voltage (tension in French) into another. Furthermore, the very process of producing electricity is a process of transforming heat and steam into electricity. We can find the word *Transformation* in at least two other contexts: in the world of finance, Transformation allows short-term savings to become long-term investments; in the steel industry, Transformation is a process of fusion of ores to make them into iron or steel. Transformation, thus, is always about the passage from one form to another. Bion uses snow as an example of the way in which water becomes a snowflake, and why—from the creation of the world until now—each snowflake is different from the next. Let's get back to EDF: its faith constitutes the second reason that could enable it to sustain and overcome the Paris–Brussels double challenge; faith, in the *Culbuto* diagram, is represented by F. Faith is sustained by doubts. There can be no faith if there are no doubts. With regards to EDF, I myself have faith in that today—thanks to the quality of the women and the men who work there, thanks to its successful praxis of Transformation, but also thanks to the positive and non-corporatist influence of trade unions, thanks to the awareness of the past and in particular of what happened to France Telecom—EDF, with a lot of zigzags, will have the capacity to take up its double challenge. But it is neither a hope, nor a blind faith.

There remains the question of the Colbertism of the French State.

Colbertism and Jacobinism are linked to a political level of interpretation, but also to a psychic one. The psychic dimension in these cases has a strong connotation of envy for another's success. In the Colbertist tradition, citizens and companies alike expect almost everything from the State. A crime of lese-majesty is thus to free oneself from the State, which partly happened with EDF. In the French culture, more than economic success, it is the fact that citizens and companies remain in a relationship of dependency *vis-à-vis* the State that matters and Electricite de France is one of the most astounding cases of an attempt to engage in an interdependent relationship. Today, EDF *must* be punished because it could spread *contagion*. The only way to avoid such a punishment is for EDF to bring to awareness and work on the process of transformation of its culture, that is to say what is most deeply within it.

*   *   *

A 15th August full of "energetic" work with EDF. Even if, looking at my notepads, I asked David Gutmann less questions than usual. Maybe through internal "avarice" on my part, almost unconsciously wanting to respect this festive day, one of the rare true "bank holidays" for a journalist, since daily newspapers are not printed on 15th August, Christmas Day, 1st May and at Easter. Or maybe because David's reasoning became rigorous, from theoretical options he moved on to practice, in the meanders of a big French public sector organization. In reality, his route is diagonally opposed: David Gutmann, through "praxis", arrives at the theory and through experience he deduces an elaboration.

I think of the misery of today's politicizing, which seeks to interpret power struggles but doesn't limit itself to reflecting on them. Without taking into consideration psychic impulse, the deep, basic tendencies that flow like rivers hidden in the entrails of a country, a culture, an economy gush out under the light of politics, surprising or even wrong-footing observers who ignored their very existence.

Without meaning to, I start to "liken" David Gutmann to other authors. I don't know her, I've never seen her, even less on television, where of course she'd rather not appear, but, for example, Barbara Spinelli is a journalist whose comments echoed those of Cocteau about mirrors "taking time to reflect before reflecting." Whether it is about Europe or the Balkans, about the secessionist push in Italy or Mediterranean issues, Barbara Spinelli, about whom I know nothing more than the fact that she lives in Paris, restitutes a meaning that is not constrained by ideologies, but loyal to the palpitation of things, whether or not it pleases the mighty ones or the readers themselves.

"Reflecting". How many times did David Gutmann use this verb with me? During telephone conversations, or here in Ostuni, during certain breaks that written conversation cannot relate, it is quite common to hear David say, "I will go and reflect on it." It is an obsolete verb, because "reflecting" in this circus of Media, whose time imposes a rhythm on our very daily life and our pleasure in talking, it is almost considered as a mistake or at least as a weakness difficult to forgive, a tedious slowness. There is something ancient, essential, beautiful in the "going to reflect", in the fact of suspending one's judgment, or one's analysis, in the wait for "insight", for a reflection that reflects the light of reality, the light of what is authentic.

I reflect upon slowness as an epistemological resource. "go slowly, think on foot" is the invitation from sociologist of knowledge Franco Cassano in his latest book Il Pensiero Meridiano, *in which the Mediterranean, the South, re-conquer the dignity of "subjects" of thinking, they don't let themselves be thought about through others' projects. Cassano, who lectures in Bari and works closely in Paris with Serge Latouche, is for me a "presence" during those days spent with David Gutmann. There are vivid resonances between the two, starting with the emphasis on "the other" inherited from Levinas, with the "solidarity against death" that Albert Camus talked about.*

A solidarity that was broken during the war in Bosnia, in the midst of the fire in the Balkans. All say that because of the thousand-year-old religious conflict between Muslims and Christians, there, like in Jerusalem, a peaceful coexistence would be impossible. Then I read an interview with Predrag Matvejevic, born in Mostar, author of Mediterraneo *and of* Mondo ex *who says: "the Yugoslav tragedy is a Shakespearian tragedy, its analysis must not be geopolitical but must focus on political genetics". In other words it is psychic. Why? Because, Matvejevic reminds us, the father of Croat leader Tudjman committed suicide, and the latter held the "communists" responsible. The father of Serbian leader Milosevic, a theologian, also killed himself, because his mother hanged herself, because his uncle hanged himself. Because still, the father of Serbo–Bosniac leader Karadzic raped a little niece and was sentenced for it. "Unconsciously, the rape never abandoned Karadzic, a psychiatrist without talent. How many women were raped in Bosnia by his militia?*

Note

1. In French, *emprise.*

CHAPTER FOUR

From envy to desire

I would like to get back to the thread of yesterday's conversation. We talked about a political dimension (the power struggles between the public administration and EDF) and a psychic dimension (the mutual dependency, imposed by Colbertism, between the State and public sector companies). There is, however, a third dimension of interpretation: the spiritual one. The first association of ideas that this third dimension suggests resonates with a religious metaphor. It is as though the State was a god who preferred to keep a hold on his worshippers rather than see them become autonomous, even though autonomy is the only way to ensure an institution's perenniality. But the State prefers to dominate its companies, even if by doing so it puts their future at risk. In France, the Republican State was built on the legacy of the Monarchy, in which the initial source of the sovereign's legitimacy is of divine origin, where the catholic influence is dominant. Some claimed, for example, that France was *the Catholic Church's eldest daughter*. The French God is protecting and domineering, whereas the Protestants' God is demanding and liberating. It isn't by chance that the *Decalogue* is made of five prohibitions and five permissions. For Catholics, the relationship with God is mediated by the priesthood; for Protestants, by the community; for Jews there is no intermediary: hence *Yom Kippur*, the day of forgiveness where Jews address God directly. In the eyes of the history of the Catholic Church, John Paul II made the mistake of entering the Society of show business.

Thus, for EDF there is a protecting and limiting God. This vision, however, needs to be put into perspective with the fact that France is a country of *mixing*: it is one of its potentials, much more than in Italy where the main dialectic is between North and South. France is a country where contradictory forces are at work, which is very positive. France's Catholic origin is still present, but the second religion is Islam, the third Protestantism, and fourth comes Judaism. In that way, Catholicism has become more and more influenced by Protestantism: we can find two million Muslims out of a population of sixty million, and France represents the fourth Jewish community in the world, after Israel, the USA, and Russia. The State itself is going through a process of Transformation, its Colbertist conception being in the middle of evolving with regards, for example, to God's infallibility—in fact to its own infallibility. Every power is an immanent and temporal—but unconscious—representation of God and of the gods. I'll tell you a Jewish riddle: "what is the difference between God and a doctor? God at least doesn't claim to be a doctor!". The psychic condition of the 'doctor-in-the-mind' is God, a protecting and limiting God.

What is, in your opinion, preferable: to be dependent and protected by God, or to take responsibility for the risks and be free?

Your question identifies an antinomy: *dependency against freedom*. Dependency gives the impression of reducing anxiety through a process of superficial change; freedom utilizes and contains the anxiety whilst enabling the difficult but creative journey of transformation.

How can we then manage the anxiety-provoking characteristic of Transformation?

Transformation is like this garden in which we're sitting, a garden full of delicacies and torments. For me, *freedom is anxiety*.

The etymology of *anxiety* can help us understand better. *Anxiety and haleter* (to pant, in English) come from the Late Latin word *"anxia, anxiare"*, which means to breathe with difficulty. But *haleter* is also to desire, so that in Latin it is the same thing to *cupere* or to *anehelare*. When anxiety, which represents desire, becomes too important, we start finding it hard to breathe with the risk of suffocation and death. Indeed we say: *I am short of breath, I am breathless*. In fact, when anxiety is not managed, in other words when the boundaries of desire do not succeed in being defined, it brings us towards death with uncontrollable breathing difficulties. Breathing *is* the heart, it is *Cupid*, desire. Therefore, the question that you are asking me is whether it is possible to master a wild beast, and if so how would that be possible. In other words, is desire controllable, and in what way? My answer is that desire cannot be tamed; however, the anxiety that is generated by desire can be managed through the creation of boundaries, such as taboos for example. It is also important to consider creativity as a form of transformation of anxiety, as is the case with sexual desire when it is transformed into a painting or a book. Or with the desire for eternity, immortality, which gets translated into a work of art, into a piece of intellectual work such as our book, into a political action that ensures Society's future or into a managerial action that renders a company performing. This is connected to Freud's concept of *sublimation*. Indeed, Transformation could be another word for what, in *psychoanalysis*, we call sublimation. Personally, I prefer to call it Transformation because this word brings with it the idea of a journey. Transformation is sublimation and *condensation*. In Freud's *Interpretation of Dreams*, condensation comes across as one of the fundamental mechanisms involved in dreaming. In chemistry, we would talk about *precipitation*. There is a *transfer* from sexual possession to the creation of a work of art. I was saying that, for me, the real question is in the relationship between freedom and anxiety and, therefore, desire. Freedom thus becomes the capacity that one develops in oneself, with the help of others, to bring to consciousness the sources of desire and, therefore, of anxiety. *The quintessence of freedom is the bringing into awareness.*

What do you mean by "consciousness" and "awareness" in this relationship to freedom?

We have within us a *black box*, which is the Unconscious and a *transparent box* which is the Subconscious.

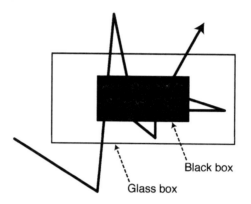

Black box, glass box and transformation.

For me, individual and collective freedom resides in the limited, temporary, daily tormented movement (*passage* in French) from unconscious to conscious, through subconscious. It is a very useful hypothesis. Why is a company successful? Because it has undergone a discernment process of the *hic et nunc*, and gained enough awareness to make action possible. These hypotheses also connect with the real definition of the role of the intellectual in Society. It is not the duty of an intellectual to become a politician or a man of action, nor is his duty to give advice to politicians or citizens. An intellectual is such a thing if he understands a little better, a little more, a little differently what desire and anxiety generate in the life of a society. An intellectual understands things, not only through the intellect, but also simultaneously through affects. So we should be talking of *intellectuals* and at the same time of *"affectuals"* or of *enlighteners*, clarifiers, and explorers. Intellectuals create and travel through *passages* from the Unconscious to the Consciousness, from unconscious to conscious. Freedom resides in this flow. Just like libido, freedom/liberty (*liberte* in French) has in fact a *liquid* origin at least as far as its Greek root *lib* goes. Freedom/liberty means to liquefy or to de-solidify, whilst to make a libation is to set off on a journey, just like a river with its cascades and its lakes. It is to render fluid. Freedom/liberty and anxiety share, with desire, this etymologic

FROM ENVY TO DESIRE   63

kinship. Transformation is the setting into motion, the flow and the clarification. Moses came out of the waters of the river Nile and of the Red Sea, Jesus walked on water and baptized with water, Minerva came out of the water, not to mention Styx. The zigzags of Transformation are like a river's loops, the meanders representing the consequences of anxiety. The Chinese talk about CHE, to describe *the propensity of things*. It is only when the force of the current becomes weaker that we can then act. When the wise man and the man of action coincide, they can tell when the current is so strong that it will prevent action from when, more rarely, the current has weakened. It is then time to act. Mao's long march is a historical testimony of this vision. A vision that we see also in the *Talmud*, in Socrates, in Plato's myth of the cave and in Sun Tsu's *Art of War*.

And even in sublimation ...

Sublimation is the passage from solid state to gas, without going through a liquid state, whereas condensation is the passage from gas to liquid. Transformation is a combination of both processes. We can then wonder why with Freud and the legacy of his thinking, that sublimation was more successful than condensation!

Maybe it's because sublimation is also the transformation of nature into culture. It is a founding process for knowledge, the arts, and the sciences.

I think that sublimation, without condensation, amounts to the production of a new understanding, but without moving into action. It represents an *insight*, but without *output*. Again, it would be interesting then to understand why sublimation was so fortunate, at the expense of condensation. In any case, free associations concerning notions of liquid and flow come to mind. The first one is about the amniotic fluid. Life in general comes out of liquid. Our body is made up of eighty per cent liquid. All the great western religions were born around the sea, the Mediterranean, and civilizations appear on the banks of rivers or the sea shores.

Take Paris, Bari, Warsaw: there is a common root—"par", "bar", "war"—which seems to be of Indo-European origin, and to mean "water".

Certainly. And let us not forget the great travels along watercourses, the Exodus with the crossing of the Red Sea, the *mare nostrum* as mother of peoples.

Sociologist Franco Cassano recently wrote that conversely totalitarian thinking is completely telluric. It belongs to the earth; it refers to Heidegger or Carl Schmitt and to a Germany that is so "central", in the European corpus, far away from the Mediterranean.

I completely agree. The earth thinking is a totalitarian thinking; by contrast the sea or water thinking is a thinking that *trades* ideas, goods, religions. It is not actually possible to *own* the sea.

But to get back to sublimation, I would say that a successful sublimation is the opposite of a displacement, because it carries with it re-introjections and an elaboration of projections. You know the famous story about a dog? A director of a company comes home angry about something that is happening at work, and he then punishes his dog. The dog consequently—after a series of events—will end up biting another man who happens to be one of his employees! Sublimation makes it possible to go home, leaving aside work-related problems, and naturally be attentive to your dog! It is the "scapegoat" that Rene Girard so magnificently described.

In the Bible, it says that scapegoats were periodically sent into the desert, all covered in dust and ashes, symbols of all of the town's sins, and that they would die in the desert, pushed, or not, off a cliff. We thus find the most vivid demonstration of the mechanism of projections from someone who doesn't work through his "sins": he banishes them outside himself, thereby having the illusion of being liberated from them. But the biblical scapegoat also represents the first steps to civilization: indeed it isn't a human now who is being sacrificed, as used to happen with the Incas, it is an animal, a goat to be precise. God stopped Abraham's hand, when out of loyalty and piety he was directing it towards his own son Isaac: a sacrificial lamb was enough. Conversely, with the Shoah, the scapegoat becomes human again: a whole people, the Jews, become the scapegoats of Hitler's Germany.

We were talking about sublimation and condensation ...

Yes, the best example of sublimation/condensation concerns death. In the face of death, there are those who fall into depression—or into megalomania, paranoia, and schizophrenia— in fact into madness. Then there are those who, to the contrary, decide to live as fully as possible in the *here and now*, creating, through their very relationships with others, becoming a poet or engineer. In fact, a human being's genius is his awareness of death transformed into an act of creation. It allows the satisfaction of his primary narcissism, all the while overcoming and transforming it. Human genius is the setting into motion of a process of genesis and of generosity. It is within his capacity to share *with*, because each intellectual, artistic, scientific, and emotional discovery can be nothing until shared with others. In the end, there is no discovery without exchange and sharing: hence the importance of tradition. Tradition and Transformation are not dissociable. Tradition in Latin is *tradere*, which means to entrust, reassure. In English, *trade* means exchange, commerce. Tradition is the succession of innovations.

Trahir *(to betray, in English), translate, transmit, tradition ... Transformation. There is always the "tran", the passage from one point to the other, as Walter Benjamin understood it in his essay "The translator's duty" which ends with these words: "All great writings must contain, in between the lines, to some extent, but more importantly for sacred scriptures, their own virtual translation. The interlinear version of a sacred text is the archetype or the ideal of every translation."*

That's how it is in the *Talmud*: the interpretation is always both a translation and a betrayal, which keeps the interpretation safe from omnipotence. The Jew—the Hebrew—is the one who is passing (from the word's Aramean origin) he is the *passer*. The *choosing* of the Jews, their originality, is located in the passing: they form a people here to pass on ideas, the monotheism, the Bible. The Jewish Easter is the passage, *Pesach* is a symbolic lamb for the Exodus from Egypt; exile is a passage, just as *Aliyah*—the *ascending*—is, in other words the collective return to the Land of Israel. Talking of *passer*, I also include it to mean a *smuggler*, working against the rigidity of borders. Translation enables betrayal. I think we should *praise betrayal*, because betrayal prevents repetition. A true successor is someone who can bring himself to betray his predecessor or genitor, because the context has changed, transformed, and what was right at the time for the predecessor isn't right any more in the successor's context. President Pompidou legitimately betrayed De Gaulle and when Chirac decided one last time to implement the madness of Mururoa, it seems that he did it to make possible an official end to all nuclear trials, not only to facilitate France's return into NATO, but especially, unconsciously, to facilitate the creation of an solely professional French army. Let us repeat that the betrayal referred to is betrayal within a Talmudic understanding, whereby every human being exists to find a new interpretation and a new action, and certainly not to repeat and reproduce successful interpretations and actions from its predecessors. Every human being has the duty of *Interpret–Action*, in other words he/she is not living his/her life truly in relation to others if he/she doesn't interpret as a means to action. Because interpretation on its own isn't enough, it must transform understanding into action for self and others, it must be *Transform–Action*. It isn't about predicting, or about being intellectualist, but about interpreting and acting in the way of Transformation. I shall quote, on the one hand, Tomasi di Lampedusa's *Leopard* with its "everything must change so that nothing changes", and, on the other, Antonio Gramsci, who for me is an admirable example of interpretation linked to action.

If the ICP has been the only communist party to overcome, almost unscathed all the while radically transforming itself, the fall of the Berlin Wall, it owes it mostly, I think, to Gramsci's lesson, in particular to the "Quaderni dal carcere" ("Notes from jail"), which makes up his political genetic. Mussolini, when in 1926, he got Gramsci arrested and sentenced to twenty years in jail, had to announce: "we must prevent this head from thinking".

Gramsci was never slave to a *mental prison*, he never behaved as a prisoner for life. He continued to think freely.

Did you know that he had been incarcerated for years, not very far from here, in Turi's prison?

I didn't, but let me tell you that the fact that we are talking about Gramsci today and here, a few miles from where he was incarcerated, doesn't seem to me to be by chance. I see the Italian communist party, called today the left democratic party (PDS) as an example of an institution in transformation.

It may be why the PCI-PDS even succeeded in "surviving" the Tangentopoli storm, the inquiries into corruption that nevertheless came too close for comfort.

Maybe. Gramsci sowed the seeds of Transformation in the PCI culture. It may even be that the presence of the Vatican in Italy helped the Italian communists to understand what an institution in transformation *is not*, and that the competition between those two *churches* was born from that difference.

*   *   *

It is a day for dictionaries. Latin and Greek. David and I dug out some ancient, torn, yellowed ones, but royal with their colourings and their quotes from translators who spent their life getting them published in Italian. They were on the little bookshelf in the barn where we work and we took them with us into the garden, under the trees, to get some fresh air. From now on they will stay by our side during those silent mornings, when all the other guests have gone to the sea (from time to time I can feel a little spike of envy on my part, sometimes on theirs!) and during those lazy, indolent afternoons, in the "controra" as we say here, in the hour "against", time during which one can only rest, sat outside the white house, under the vine, looking at the "nothing" and renaming it with passing thoughts. There is the one who answers Plato and the one who answers Adam. Benjamin, who today—with his hand on his forehead and his light and round glasses just like Gramsci's—was present with his reflections on translation, said that it was Adam who invented Philosophy. Because Adam, first man and "father of names", created reality with language, with the intimate identity between a thing and its name, a secret music, which loses its tune or even gets lost itself when we try to separate an essence from the word that expresses it. It is the language that at the beginning (and at the end) is always a biblical language, the word of God.

David Gutmann is fascinated by words, by etymologies, by connections, and by psycholinguistic affinities that emerge between one term and another. He seemed almost keen, earlier on, to modify the course of his discourse, to follow a significance that would confirm a signification, to discover the uncertain traces of a word, to the point where he could have caught a glimpse of its genesis, of Genesis.

Even his availability for authors different from one another and a lot further even from his own background, such as Gramsci, surprises me. They have been "adopted" by the Transformation-Approach because of their vitality, of a duality that is not complaisance, but disposition for understanding in order to act. This attention, I would describe as filled with solidarity, vis-à-vis Mandela or Gramsci, prisoners of a regime, but not of the mental prison in which, however, so many "free" men find themselves.

Life is David's main question. The motto of "living and not surviving" (vivre et non survivre) *moves through these days and this book, which accompanies men and women in the passage of Transformation, which illuminates the road like a star. And behind this star, there is another one, the Star of David, which Nazis used to sew onto their victims' jackets, in Auschwitz, in Buchenwald, in Dachau. David Gutmann is the son of a woman who survived the extermination camps and he wouldn't even have been born if Hitler hadn't exterminated his father's first family. It is an idea that I don't think, it simply arrives and paralyses me like a shiver of cold, which I disregard immediately, first of all out of respect for my interlocutor, for his pain, and then out of sheer horror. But that's the way it happened. So yes I "think". I try to think about a child who grows up and who doesn't know anything about his father's "other" life, and yet he "knows" it just like sailors' sons "know" that the sea is tormented even if they were born and live far away from the shore. He knows it "inside", in the psyche, in the genes. I try to think about this child's feeling of guilt, a child who could have not been called David Gutmann, and I think about the alternative that he's had to face: to choose "guilt" and to survive or to choose "meaning" and to live.*

"Choose life and not death," you can read in the first "mitzvah", Talmudic law's fundamental precept. And David Gutmann keeps this deep within him. But he doesn't limit himself to defend it in the darkness of a millennial casket, he brings it to the light, to the limelight, he rationalizes it and details it. Because we, from this "complicated" century, we are not only children of the Bible, we are also Freud's children, and he advocated the irrationality of the unconscious, but the rationality of the study of the unconscious. The soul is now called psyche. The twentieth century saw the sin of the Shoah and didn't manage to avoid the even more horrible sin of repression of this crime against humanity.

"Living and not surviving" thus becomes an arduous art shared with others which, co-substantial to man, becomes the daily science of our lived world. It is the imperative of a child who has become an adult and has given another name to his fear. He found the courage and called it "Transformation". He tells me it and I don't fear its contamination, I like to welcome it into my dictionary.

CHAPTER FIVE

Manager of oneself

*H*ow can one, in the chaos of everyday life, orientate oneself towards Transformation, a chaos that appears, evermore, to represent reality?

It is important to point out that the Orient is so important to the Occident that it has led the latter to invent the word *orientate*. The Orient, therefore, is the archetypal other. To orientate oneself, in keeping with Lacan, is to find one's direction in relation to the other. As for chaos' latency, it is linked to anxiety and leads us to permanent responses, which is a mistake. If we adopt, in contrast, a partial and punctual clarification of the *here and now* in our relation with others, we will then remain, well and truly, in a world of imperfection and, therefore, in one of Transformation. Any univocal or permanent response means the end of the journey of Transformation and places us in the unidimensionality that Marcuse talks about. But life is complex and *plural* and the various contacts that we have within it are like streams that come and feed our thirst. Each stream has its own taste, a consistency different to that of others, and corresponds to different requirements at various stages within our life. Going even further, if you and I drank from the same jug of water, that water would have a different flavour for each of us, depending on whether it had been drank out of vital necessity or simply out of desire, and so on. One must, therefore, conclude that it is the receptor that creates the transmitter, just as the demand creates the supply. But, in a system of *mental prison*, receptor and transmitter are prisoners of each other, of their respective projections. That is the worst of all prisons.

To seek responses that are permanent is equivalent to occulting Death, which means giving it the role of unique protagonist and submitting oneself to it. Here, we revisit the idea of scapegoat: bringing someone else to death as a way of avoiding to see ourselves as mortal. When, for example, a company puts its poor results down to the Government's failings, it shuts down its opportunity of working on itself, even if the public authorities are actually to blame. Indeed, what is most important is *to sweep up one's own front yard*, something that I have seen done here in the villages of South Italy. Let's take another example. When Mrs Thatcher threw herself wholeheartedly into the Falklands war against Argentina, a war that caused thousands to die, she did it to avoid confronting herself with the United Kingdom's real problems. The Falklands became the *Fakelands*, the lands of deception. There exists an ontological mystery of life and death, by that I mean the mystery of one's own life and one's own death. Entropic responses to this mystery are either projections (mainly projections that have not been processed) or mysticism, sects, Zen philosophy as totalitarian ideology, Tantrism chosen as *the* absolute practice, taking refuge in myths, in other words *trance*-formation, which is precisely not Transformation. Transformation is actually one of the responses to *trance*-formation. Or to be more accurate: Transformation is probably the best way, the most constructive way, to respond to *trance*-formation, in other words to the formation of trance, of states that may be spectacular or plain, but always have to do with flight.

This is a ferocious critique of sectarian spiritualism or other easy mysticisms that are in fashion nowadays, and which sometimes advocate some forms of hypnosis or even real trances.

Nazism and fascism were trances. Padania's independence from Italy that Umberto Bossi, the leader of the Lega Nord, talks about is a trance. There are also, however, the more banal trances of everyday life: arguments in a couple, making workers redundant, strike action, or even Bossi's desire to lead one million people to the banks of the river Po ... Trances are chaos popping its head up in the process of transformation, and as such we can't stop it from happening. It is rather preferable to intervene when there is still time to do so; not heavily, but enough to show that there are psychic and physical boundaries. These boundaries need to be marked out; a few embankments need to be raised to prevent manifestations of chaos from turning into madness. I will quote, as an example, the month of July 1996, in Israel, in Jerusalem, when a terrible demonstration from Israeli fundamentalists, which led to a counter-demonstration from Laics, brought about an extremely harsh intervention from the police and a diminishment of the boundary between chaos and madness. A few days later, a second demonstration took place, and was, in contrast, the focus of a work of interpretation, which consequently led to a discrete police presence, a presence that was primarily about setting clear mean-ingful boundaries: chaos that time did not degenerate into madness.

So it is about a work of what in therapy we would call "containment", but also of "management" of social processes. Can both practices ever coincide?

To think or to say that individuals can be the object of a *management* process is a fundamental error: it is almost a crime. How could it be possible? They are not objects they are subjects. When we talk about the *management* of individuals, we are in fact talking about their *manipulation*. True *management* is about offering, establishing, and making available the necessary conditions and resources for individuals to be managers of themselves, to govern themselves. The word *management* has French—and not English— origins, with Italian and Latin roots. It comes from *manege* (meaning an enclosure in which horses learn to ride). *Le Ménage des Champs* written by a Frenchman, Olivier de Serres at the end of the nineteenth century, was the first book on management. It marks the birth of modern agronomy. I'd like to think that the etymology of the word *management* is *mens agree*. Whether it is true or not, I am inviting you to consider it as right! The only *management* that can succeed is the one that *procures* and *creates with* the conditions and the resources so that people can act consciously, whilst using both their intellect and their affect. Thus, we see the quality of the one who is co-author. Since *auctor* is the basis for *auctoritas*. Managing, from a political point of view, enables the co-creation of the conditions and resources for the work, true joint management in fact! From a psychic point of view, the main role of management is precisely one of "containment": a competent manager is someone who knows how to and can contain insufficiently.

Is this quality for containment also part of your work as consultant?

Absolutely. In relation to the fibrillation, uncertainty, and anxiety that are part of the search for freedom, the main part of my role—and I say this on the basis of my experience—is really about "containment". In other words the capacity to transform physical and psychic projections, coming from without and within institutions, so that my work and that of others can continue in positive terms for the institution itself. Every institution is subjected to *incitements* and *excitements*, formulated respectively by the inside and by the outside. Incitements and excitements are seen as aggressions, because they cause the pre-established order to derail and arouse, consequently, the institution's homeostasis (the system's return to a previous order). In that case, the "containment" operated by the manager can serve as both a reassuring function and a process that discriminates true aggressions from imaginary ones. The manager's "containment" is a personal quality that nevertheless cannot be exercised without being shared, since there is no saviour nor hero.

In Bertolt Brecht's words, "Blessings on the people that needs no hero".

A hero or so-called hero is bound to revolve in a *Saviour–Victim–Persecutor* circle: his destiny, from then on, is a catastrophe for him and for others. Problems start when Zorro arrives! The experience of everyday life makes me think that it is not the situation that creates a saviour, but the saviour that creates a situation for rescuing. The role of containment can be found as easily in a couple as in the State, including a company. The most crucial of all managements is *the management in the mind*, and therefore *the containment in the mind*. Managers are producers of containment—and first of all of their own containment—thus allowing a positive process of identification on the part of others, working with them on their own capacities to govern themselves. Etymologically, to contain comes from *cum tenere*: to hold together. Containment can only derive from a collective and shared process, one that includes, of course, the leader of that process in the sharing.

Hierarchy is, therefore, necessary, is it?

Hierarchy is useful when it allows for the new leaders, in terms of containment, to replace the old ones, to appear on the scene whilst taking into consideration the circumstances of incitement as well as excitement. In a war, if a commanding officer gets killed, it will most likely be his second in command who will take his place. In a less warlike context—such as aggressions from competitors—a company will mobilize some of its sub-systems to implement a containment process. The etymology of *tenir* (to hold) also suggests very well how containment enables duration, persistence, and the maintenance of vigour. There is an intimate relationship between containment and an institution's dynamism. There you see the metaphor of Transformation as an internal combustion engine, which works according to the compression and explosion principle.

Are there dangers associated with containment or its excesses?

The dangers reside in a manager's specific temptation, when receiving projections from others, to convert containment into repression. From retention to repression, there is a risk of too quick a shift. Managers are the focus of internal and external projections and are the object of a request that one could summarize by the words "reassure us". They are being asked for over-assurance that withdraws freedom from organizational members. Such is the dictators' secret: the regression towards infancy of individuals who then rely completely on them. But one must acknowledge that to be an adult is difficult. Part of the regression—in the transformation process—comes from this real difficulty, which must be respected, and not despised. The role of the leader, and that of the manager, is to take into account the harshness of being adult, to enable infantile regression in others to be expressed, without deriving pleasure from it or feeding one's greed for power.

Where is the boundary between containment and repression, or even compression?

There is no *a priori* answer. In the moment, it is very difficult to grasp the difference. Containment ensures a kind of calm and determination, whereas compression generates rigidity and stubbornness. However, it is very subjective. The difference can only truly be grasped through the affects. In my mind containment maintains and at the same time develops freedom, whilst compression comes across as a hermetic barrier, blocking the freedom's current, its flow. Containment can be symbolized by the banks of a river, which stop its water from overflowing, but do not slow down its current. Compression, by contrast, is like a dam that obstructs the water, stops it, and leaves it to stagnate or seethe. Furthermore, containment is a factor that enables and increases creativity and therefore, creation. In a company, the preamble to containment is the alliance between those that I would describe as the *mad Entrepreneurs*, the *reasonable Entrepreneurs*, and the *reasoned Bureaucrats*. We have, conversely, the collusion of compression which seals an agreement between the *fanatical Bureaucrats*, the *reasoned Bureaucrats* and the *reasonable Entrepreneurs*, through expelling the *mad Entrepreneurs* and also after a while the *reasonable Entrepreneurs*. Containment produces innovation whilst compression generates inhibition. In some cases regression enables further progression, in others regression, conversely, brings about repression.

Could you give us an example, to make these concepts a bit more concrete?

Certainly. I am thinking, for example, about the immigration policy in France or in Italy. What is immigration? It is putting to the test a country's capacity for containment. The temptation is not laxity, which in turn would be a mistake, but compression–repression.

However, the more barriers there are to immigration, the more violent and destructive the explosion to come will be, whether it is in the country of asylum or in the country of origin. The Great Wall of China was met with real success, simply because it was unique in history and during a limited period. Here, we can't stop the *Barbarian invasion*. Nowadays, in our countries, we have to face three issues: Aids, lethal drug-use, and in particular, crack and the exclusion of youths, particularly those of minority ethnic groups. The danger is not outside any more—communism, it is worth noting, is resisted in three countries that all start with the letter C: Cuba, China, and Korea (Coree in French)!—but inside. The boiling over in suburban areas, as it was so crudely shown in the film *La Haine*, suggests an *internal* peril in resonance with immigration. This is one of the main challenges for democracy: how to contain the internal and external exclusion of immigrants? The responses that democratic States will be able to offer this exclusion will put to the test democracy's actual capacities for containment. Neither can we rely only on the hope of resolving the issue. Hope very often becomes one of the most dangerous elements. The [French] proverb says it: hope makes you live. It is literally so: hope creates despair, since being in despair requires that one has experienced hope before. Hope is useful insofar as it is achievable, but then it is not hope any more!

But if we avoid feeding our hopes, which are equivalent, in some ways, in sociological terms, to revealed and thereby dangerous expectations, what is left to a society in terms of envisaging the future?

What's left is Faith. Not in a religious sense, but in a civil, laic, and much larger sense. If a society is really in the flux of a transformation, with the zigzags that it entails, that society and its members acquire a bit more well-being than unease, a bit more success than failure, a bit more health that ill-health. And still, a bit more freedom than dependence, maturity than infantilism, capacity to ask itself questions than finding ready-made answers, and finally a bit more capacity to live its desire in relation to lack.

Containment or repression? How does one get to understand whether an organization is promoting creativity within its core?

There can be no creativity solely within an organization, because it would be like depriving fire of oxygen: the fire dies out. Oxygen is the exchange with the outside. Let's take music for example. What we call *World Music* shows that the symbolic universe evolves faster than society. It demonstrates that western music has fortunately created hybrids with other sounds, in a transformation process. Don't forget: we are not talking about a synthesis but a hybridizing, a third form. The concept of *hybrid* is one that is closest to the reality of the other. In a hybrid you have two different beings that give life to a third one, different from the first two. In the animal kingdom, hybrids can't have any descendants. In my mind, by contrast, amongst humans hybrids are probably the most generative of all. Let's get back to Faith; we are very much talking about a process of transformation, and not about a belief: loyalty to the process of transformation that cannot but be shared with others. Whilst on that topic, could we talk about the importance that I give to the game of rugby in the Transformation-Approach?

Rugby?! With you Mister Gutmann, there is no shortage of surprises . . .

Rugby, to which American football is very close, has played a big role in the comprehension and the working out of my concept of Transformation. And this is not simply because I played rugby in my youth, or because I prefer it to football, but for other reasons. In rugby there is, for a start, a way of scoring points called, in French, transformation (conversion in English). But also the shape of the ball, which in rugby is different to any other, is important: a rugby ball looks like the Earth, but more importantly, you never know in which direction it will go when it touches the ground. Because of its very shape, a rugby ball's trajectory is unpredictable. The unpredictable character of a football comes from the way it is touched. This too is the case with a rugby ball, but the latter has something more: its impact on the ground renders it unpredictable. In fact, a rugby ball generates zigzags. Perhaps a powerful computer could predict its trajectory, but it would be too late, beyond the actual playing of the game. The beauty of rugby comes from its unpredictable aspect, which we also see in the *transformation* (conversion) of the try, which constitutes a plus—as it is the case in football too, a penalty isn't in itself an advantage, it still needs to be *transformed* into a goal. In rugby, a try is worth five points, but a transformed/converted try is worth seven. Rugby was invented by the English, devoid of a Cartesian mind we are told, who made a vice of necessity, but what a pleasant one!

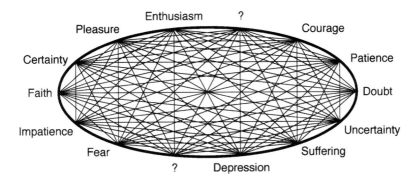

Affects (the rugby ball).

... in rugby, there are regressions, through the ball escaping the player's total control. It is the ball of anti-omnipotence, in a game that can be interpreted in very different ways (South Africa's national team, for example, used to play a massive game that veered towards omnipotence in the controlling of the ball, whereas New Zealand plays a game that is a lot more open to unpredictability).

Many are those who consider rugby to be a violent sport.

Rugby is just like bullfighting: you either like it or you don't. The game involves power and elegance. Great rugby teams are therefore aesthetic, but also ethical. Violence comes from either the grip of resistances, or from the struggle against those resistances. In the latter case the violence is transforming. There is a violence that comes from the widening of knowledge, on the road to freedom, in the passing from unconscious to conscious; and even in that context, there are moments of radical destruction, because of course we couldn't have convinced Hitler, we should have killed him. There is, equally, the violence of a *saviour's* action: a violence that serves no purpose in the extension of understanding. I am talking about the *heroes'* violence, the violence of Marat or Lenin, the proletarian avant-garde's violence, which maintains and reinforces a process of dependence. Take Vaclav Havel's velvet revolution, which was, in fact, a revolution of the passage from fanatical to measured, in other words a transformation. Finally, in every human being there remains, with regards to the issue of violence, a small amount of free will, with only one taboo: that of the destruction of humanity.

You are referring to the genocide, I imagine.

Yes, the intolerable appears when humankind or a part of humankind is threatened by extinction.

This taboo was even transgressed at Hiroshima.

I don't agree. The aim of the Americans, when they dropped those atomic bombs on Hiroshima and Nagasaki, was not to destroy all the Japanese. Added to that the fact that the use of those nuclear weapons might have prevented, in all likelihood, the use of new atomic weapons after that. A boundary was established.

Can I submit an objection though? Not on a historical level but on a metaphysical one, does every human being not represent the whole of humankind?

I don't know what to say to that. To understand does not necessarily mean to forgive, to explain can never mean to justify. We are facing the scandal of physical and psychic suffering, which is impossible to accept.

Elsa Morante would have called it the scandal of history.

Yes, taking into account that human imperfection requires one to never stop exposing scandal, and to choose within oneself and with others to diminish, be it in an infinitesimal way, the manifestations of that scandal.

*   *   *

I wasn't expecting the rugby bit. The entire afternoon was spent explaining the rules of this game that I knew nothing about. In the barn's garden today his wife, his sons, Maritè, come and go. There is sweetness, but also a bit of tension around us who are working. There is the fear to disturb but also the curiosity. There are authentic feelings, with the ambivalence that goes with them and which must be grasped, understood, transformed. I can feel that my outlook will never be the same again after these few days spent with David Gutmann. Is this a statement that appears ridiculous or the fruit of a fascination for the "guru"? But such is not the case. I did not get struck by lightening on the road to Damascus. I am not about to embrace a theory; I share with David no ideology and our respective experiences are very different from each other. My encounter with him is, precisely, an encounter with "the other". An encounter which up to now has even been marked with difficulties, of a long "transaction" about the means and the stages of our joint work. With my impatience following certain phone calls from the very kind Mrs Bertolini, the Forum's secretary. These communications in proper Italian signalled each time the absence of David's voice, when I wanted to speak to him. But the "other" is like that: he has his own schedule; he even has his own mental journeys and naturally has his own failings. Sometimes he has no answer, like following my question today about Hiroshima. David stopped "playing" with his pipe for a few minutes and then he said to me: "I don't know what to say to that". Luckily not all answers are waiting for us, and luckily not all questions are ready to be formulated. In this long interview, even journalism avoids the delirium of omnipotence, of the "truth live" and sees itself for what it really is: a daily activity of approximation of the facts and of their provisional interpretation, in a climate of often contradictory items of news, of uncontrollable sources given the distance or the haste, of institutions and cultures that beseech observations "on the field".

Journalists are often not courageous enough—a cowardice they call "objectivity"—to develop some self-awareness, or at least an awareness of the part of themselves that counts in every news story, "here and now", in the questions that they ask, in the tales that they restitute. There is, only sometimes, a professional witness' narcissism—the "I was there"—that signals the personality of the one who is writing. But what about their secret dramas, their past, and their present? Great articles in suffering and in hope, from John Reed to Oriana Fallaci, stir the reader, by contrast, with something completely different, and by that I mean co-participation, compassion, indignation, and utopia from the one who is writing. No question is neutral: to know that is already doing a nice favour to the article one is about to write. If you write in one page about the crisis of fatherhood or about the drama of a psychiatric asylum, would you or would you not tell your experience of having an authoritarian or absent father, a parent with mental health problems? And if you have nothing, truly nothing in your life, if you are "clean" like a sheet of white paper, in your pages will there not seep in between the lines, maybe sometimes, this white that erases everything? In other words: why write if you have neither joy nor pain? Is it a technique? An abstraction?

Some of the words used today in my interview with David— spirituality, mysticism—are very real, for example, in my relationship with Maritè. I know it and David Gutmann knows it too. We don't talk about it, that's not what we are here for, but it is like when you write a script. Writers know about the past of characters in a film, even if they only describe them in the present. To give a character a past, a conscience (and an unconscious), parents, brothers and sisters, in other words a human baggage, helps to better define him in the relationships, in the dialogues, in the actions on screen. And if it works for fiction ...

Even David Gutmann isn't exempt from it. One of his sons, on his return to Paris, will have to have a leg operated on. Annie fell off a horse and she badly hurt her knee. The other two sons, in the space of forty-eight hours, came to see their father, whilst we were working, to show him grazes on their legs and ask him what they should do. David reassured them and then said to me: "they are all preoccupied with their brother, and they are all hurting their legs to remember and to remind me that there is an operation in prospect". It is an observation that can appear banal, but only if it is taken within the context of "non-existent coincidences". By that I mean that, in my case, I hadn't thought of it.

CHAPTER SIX

Murderous projections

When projections are not processed, they can become violent and extremely destructive. When we talk about mechanisms of transference and counter-transference, we can be fooled into thinking that they are just big words, for intellectuals, and have nothing to do with reality, with the impact and the force of facts. But that is not exactly true. One day I was asked to intervene in the psychiatric department of an Italian local health unit (LHU). I intervened using an Institutional Transformation methodology. Periodically over several days, I met, simultaneously or successively, all the LHU members, from the porter to the medical director, with the only exception being the small team responsible for emergency interventions. So we organized a first plenary session with all the members of the Department. On arrival, I realize that the chairs are laid out in a complete mess. Similarly the way in which individuals start speaking, one after the other, is in a disjointed or incoherent way, the discussion appears to be following anyone's goodwill. Then a description emerges, through the participants, of a department made up of anarchical cells, impossible to regulate and with a tendency to proliferate, putting at risk the department's very existence. It would appear that only the medical director is choosing to resist this "corruption" phenomenon. Now a revelation is made that he has just found out that he has cancer, and that he is being treated for it outside his territory.

I then volunteered that the description of the organization portrayed by its members is similar to the structure of a cancer. Stupor engulfs the room and in the "space" of a few minutes the comprehension of my working hypothesis becomes manifest. The medical director is both silent and pale. A few people, the majority of them women, start crying. Other people, mostly men (!), claim that my hypothesis is absurd. I ask them if by any chance ... they want to confine me! More seriously, I share the following hypothesis that the organization's cancer has been projected and transferred onto the person who leads it. In my hypothesis, I am being particularly supported by the members of the lowest levels of the hierarchy, such as the porters and the nursing auxiliaries. We can formulate the hypothesis that each of us has the potential to develop cancer, but that circumstances trigger or not the development of the disease. In this particular case, we can talk of a collusion between an institution and its leader, who will offer himself in sacrifice, taking the cancer within himself—in an unconscious way—to save in vain the institution.

But it could also perfectly be the reverse process: the leader's cancer is transferred onto the organization.

We could, it is true, take into consideration the reverse process: the projection of the director's physiological cancer onto his organization. In the *here and now* of the intervention, that hypothesis didn't come to my mind and I didn't feel its resonance inside me. Whether one or the other of the hypotheses is valid, or even other ones, a year and a half on—in August 1996—thanks to quality of treatment, to the personal determination of the patient–director, and *maybe* to the Institutional Transformation intervention, the director is still alive and appears to be, if not cured, at least in a much better state.

Your hypothesis of a "reverse process" is very interesting. When a destructive phenomenon is created, it mutually feeds itself from its different sources. Which came first: the chicken or the egg? It doesn't matter. Getting a transformation process going helps, once again, not so much to prevent the regression—which is impossible —but to stop it before this regression–destruction becomes irreversible. Cancer is the negation of death. It takes the form of an anarchical development of cells that can't die, and which in that way destroy the whole organism. It is the same with atomic fusion: neutrons de-multiply in an infinite chain. The phenomenon of life is cell division: a cell dies to give birth to two cells, and when the division stops you have death. Cancer refuses death. Cells no longer reproduce by dividing, but by multiplying, by the malignant metamorphosis of sane cells. Cancer is an example of totalitarian transformation, without regulation or containment. A metaphor for cancer is: "Negating death is the safest way of inducing it, in a regression process dominated by hysteria and suffering". Refusing death is equivalent to inducing it either in a spectacular way—"the thousand years of the third Reich", cancer, nuclear fusion—or through the banality of everyday life, when it evolves in the repetition of, in effect, a vegetal existence. In other words, when someone is no longer the co-author of the transformation of his or her life. This sadly happens to too many a person.

Have you had confirmation of this "disease as metaphor" that Susan Sontag had also talked about? Have you met other examples of it in your work?

Yes, in the course of another intervention that we concluded after four years of working on it. My colleagues and I intervened in one of the world's biggest cancer treatment centres. I worked, in particular, with the director of the centre, as well as with a group of a dozen of people in their forties who, within a few years, are likely to become the directors of the centre. Several months from the start of the intervention, a truly astounding working hypothesis began to emerge. Our intervention, in fact, shines light on the fact that the organization of this centre—including its spatial organization, its working methods, its management—instead of helping its staff to better intervene technically and psychically, renders the work more difficult. We sensed, in addition, a great deal of suffering from staff at the different levels of the centre: amongst administrative as well as medical and paramedical staff, amongst nurses as well as doctors, researchers as well as surgeons. This suffering at work appears very understandable given the disease they are treating: cancer. And indeed, that's what it's about, since the most difficult cases present to this centre, and consequently there are a high proportion of failed treatments and a greater difficulty in caring for patients. A complementary study with the centre's catholic chaplain enables us to go further in the comprehension–revelation: the presence and the intensity of this suffering were hardly explored in the centre. They were not even explicitly verbalized despite the fact that it was a cancer treatment centre, and not a television-manufacturing centre. In fact this suffering, the unexpressed and unprocessed failures (in parallel with the successes), lead to a feeling of guilt, which drove the organization to self-punishment. It is for that reason that management increased the strain at work rather than easing it. The hypothesis is astounding.

What happened when you communicated your hypothesis to those concerned, to the senior managers?

In the group of those in their forties, the resistances were not too strong, because the working hypothesis had been constructed with them. But when the working group presented the hypothesis to the centre's senior managers, the resistances and the reaction were of an extraordinary violence. During the meeting when the hypothesis was presented, and especially afterwards, the various senior managers besieged the director in his office and even in his home. So much that late one night, the director rang me to ask me if we shouldn't stop the intervention as his closest colleagues were demanding we be fired, calling us *barking mad*. Chance, or rather a true premonition, had led us to include, right from the start, the director in the working group of those in their forties, himself the only one in his sixties. In talking to him, he confirmed to us that had he not taken part in the working group, he would have given in to the pressures from the other senior managers.

Finally, after much hesitation, he decided to continue. Transformation was thus able to continue its course and was translated into a certain amount of practical decisions that, without a doubt, allowed the organization of the work in the centre to become less punitive. But a few months later, the director developed cancer. The work that I did specifically with him, then, was to show how a director, from the moment when he fights against the mortifying repetition of his institution, ends up receiving destructive projections that can lead to the putting at risk of his psychic and physical integrity. The director, who is now retired, was treated in his centre and recovered three years later. In addition, when he retired, we made it very clear that we would leave with him. This case shows that in an Institutional Transformation intervention, it is essential to hold on tight, until the very passage of transformation is reached. Here it was the revelation of the working hypothesis, according to the following logic: (1) an unavoidable suffering, albeit unprocessed; (2) a sense of blame and guilt; (3) self-punishment; and (4) hurt and hurtful management.

Had the director not been confident about the necessity of this passage represented by the revelation of the interpretation, the resistances would have won and the regression would have been a lot stronger than the disappointment.

Did you derive theoretical consequences from this?

The concept of hurtful and self-punishing management was for me one of the truly surprising discoveries in this work with a cancer treatment centre. In the past, we had conceived the idea of an absent, or distant, management, particularly during one of our interventions with the Catholic Church, amongst orders and congregations of the regular clergy.

Can you clarify what it is that you are referring to?

I have become aware that there is a very deep and unconscious tendency amongst ecclesiastical orders and congregations, whether they are made up of men or of women, to elect to positions of responsibility at any level (convent, novitiate, province, general superiors), those who are, in effect, least able to take on the management duties of their institution. Management thus becomes distant or even absent and not only for geographical reasons. Through working, for the last seven years now, in conferences that gather those in charge of congregations and orders, as well as the general superiors of a few congregations, I have come to this working hypothesis. Absent or distant management in the monastic world of the Catholic Church is a reaction against the hyper-hierarchies of its secular part (Vatican, Pope, Cardinals, Arch-bishops ...); the only exception coming from Jesuits, who don't have their "black pope" by chance. We have there a phenomenon of both institutional and unconscious compensation.

If we could come back for a minute to the self-punishing management, this discovery was made in the context of hospital life, but we can use it to understand other institutions too. For example, in the western world, there are no independent arms manufacturing industries left. They all went bankrupt, such as the arms manufacturers in Saint-Etienne, or they lost a lot of money and have been absorbed by other companies. Some merged with industrial groups that also produce civilian goods, others have themselves created "compensating" civilian departments, the F. N. Herstal in Belgium combining several of those processes. It would appear to me that, for reasons that are similar to those of the cancer treatment centre, manufacturing weapons for war is very guilt-inducing, especially in a Christian society. Even more so when these feelings of guilt are not being explored, which can lead either to a harmful management, or to a drowning of the issue of military production into the ocean of civilian production.

This reflection is not the fruit of cheap morals; it aims at signalling to what extent the unconscious can be destructive when it doesn't choose to be elaborated on. We could link this to a famous saying from Montaigne: "Science without conscience only ruins the soul". Action without the constant work of developing awareness can lead individuals, as well as institutions, down the road of entropy, and not on the path to Transformation. So that responsibility does not so much reside in the respect of one's own actions than in the willingness to understand why we engage in those actions. *Responsibility becomes not so much for the consequences, but for the causes of our actions.* Etymologically, responsibility is the fact of being able to respond (to a problem). To be more precise, responsibility resides in the formulation of the problem rather than in the response. You may remember Woody Allen retorting: "I've found the answer, but could you remind me the question!", because if a question brings an opening, an answer only blocks it off.

*   *   *

*Sunday. This morning, excursion, yahoo! For the first time since David
and his family are here in Ostuni, we too have left the barn, the garden, the
dialogue sustained on two voices. Two couples, all friends, are with us.
One is the psychiatrist Pina Labellarte, who introduced me to David
Gutmann, and her husband Mario de Pasquale, who almost twenty years
ago was my philosophy teacher at college. I have felt, ever since, a real
affection for his capacity to teach with lightness, to learn, and to make
people learn with irony. The others are two friends of Mario's and Pina's,
and of David's, and they are, in contrast, not very familiar to me. And of
course, I am in the company of Maritè.*

*We go to Alberobello, inland, the magical region of the "trulli", very
old dwellings made completely out of stones, with a characteristic conic
roof. Then, we eat on the coast, and wander through two villages of blue
and white, lime and sea, Monopoli and Polignano. From time to time, as
we turn into deserted little streets in this dead hour of a Sunday in
August, I have the feeling that I have just walked into a scene from
Bunuel's "Discreet charms of the bourgeoisie". Surreal! Everybody is
either eating watermelon or dozing on the beach, and we, we are here on a
walk, talking about the Latin etymology of the word "peril" . . . I have the
distinct impression that what he is seeing for the first time though, the
beauty of the landscape or of the architecture matter little to David, that
they are only the object of a hasty look. I think that he does not want to
waste time and that he has work on his mind. Even I don't feel at ease.
These are places that I know really well and love, but today I almost feel
disorientated. In the emotional space or in the exclusive that was created in
my daily work with David, I have lost the habit, perhaps, of contacts, even
superficial ones, with other people. And even at the start of the afternoon, if
on one hand I would like to prolong these hours of distractions, on the
other I think that it would be preferable to return to the garden as soon as
possible.*

*We are there now. David is talking of cancer this afternoon. Of life and
death. I ask fewer questions than usual. I am starting to feel uncomfortable.
We are finishing, the evening is already well on its way. A candelabrum is
brought to us so that we can continue to take notes. A "gothic"
premonition: during the night, I don't feel well, to the point that I'm
thinking about calling a doctor. Maritè is frightened and I try to reassure
her, despite the stomach pains, the obvious fruit of an accumulation of*

anxiety (last night's twelve dishes over dinner at the barn were incredibly light). I sleep very little. The following morning, when Maritè and Annie go to Bari to do some shopping and photocopy the notes taken up to now, I leave my hotel and make my way apprehensively to the barn. I stop to buy a new notepad and I pay no attention to the front cover illustration before getting back into the car. On the pad there is a horrible dragon spitting out fire, an "alien" with eyes full of blood, diabolical horns and very sharp claws. There is even a large inscription: "visions of the night" and underneath a sentence written in smaller cases: "welcome to the dark side of your mind. It is terrific! It is yours". I think straightaway, in a Pavlovian type response, about the censorship that is sometimes necessary. Such images should never be on the cover of notepads that are then bought by children and adolescents. But seconds later I am already thinking that this dragon came to find me last night and that now it is here, to remind me of its existence, which by now is reduced to the position of icon. I will immediately talk to David about it, who this morning mentions, first of all, the existence of two different time zones. The "Ostuni time" is mine, always a bit late due to traffic and the appearing of dragons. The "Dourdan time" is the time of the conferences organized by the International Forum for Social Innovation that take place in a little town near Paris, his of course being more punctual. He is right but it doesn't minimize this "criticism"—in any case that is how I experience it—and I get a bit surly.

We were talking about yesterday and about the bad night I spent and David Gutmann inscribed it into the text that we had been writing: "it is a regression—he argues—that enables us to go forward. Had you decided to go to casualty, since it was only an expression of anxiety or had you decided, this morning, to give up the work, the regression would have become insurmountable. But it didn't win, it is you who triumphed over it in your itinerary of transformation and of creativity with me.

It may have nothing to do with it, but after yesterday's Bunuel I am now remembering Zavattini's Miracle in Milan (talking about journey, an author who "weaved reality") and De Sica. It is the last bit of dialogue in the film, when the bells fly off from the Duomo square towards a land where "Good day! really means good day".

So, Ostuni or Dourdan, dragon or no dragon, after all this morning I too say: good day.

CHAPTER SEVEN

With Moses in the company

*P*rofessor Gutmann, yesterday we talked about your intervention in
a cancer treatment centre. Have you worked with medical or
research institutions that deal with Aids?

No, I haven't. From a symbolic as well as strictly medical point
of view, Aids is an acquired disease, cancer, conversely, is an
endogenous disease. During those two experiences that I talked to
you about yesterday, the two directors were wrestling in favour of
Transformation in a context that is "guaranteed" by the consultant.
Some institutions die of institutional cancer. It is, then, the most
difficult of situations for those, in a way, who "carry the
transformation", and in particular for the directors of these
institutions.

*In a lovely passage, Elias Canetti declares: "Predator of mourning,
man". Can we give it the flavour of the day and say: "Predator of
mourning, institution"?*

When we try to promote a process of transformation in a
mortifying and entropic institution and when the violence of

resistances goes beyond anything one can imagine, the danger is great. There are moments of extreme madness. The danger lies in the fact that the co-authors of Transformation put themselves—and are placed—in the role of the saviour, and this in response to the unconscious request for omnipotence. Hence at times, it is better to drop everything, to accept impotence, temporarily or definitely. Every leader becomes a "container", a receptacle for projections. Container and receptacle are two similar concepts, although they are also quite different. If the projections one receives are too strong, if the leader is a passive receptacle that does not—with the others— process projections, he won't be able to become a "container". By definition, the "container" is someone who lives the process of "containment" and he is an active, conscious receptacle that shares the work of processing projections. The destiny of a "receptacle", conversely, is to explode, as we see in the final scene of Antonioni's *Zabriskie Point*. This explosion happens within a process of progressive paralysis, of sterilization, of drowsiness, of "uncon-scious", in both meanings of the word. The "container" is like the concrete mixer on a lorry. The lorry is driving and at the same time the concrete mixer is rotating. The concrete-mixer lorry gets its energy from the outside (diesel) and it needs drivers who alternate and take over from one another behind the wheel. Furthermore, the lorry must be periodically serviced. In mortifying institutions, the co-authors of Transformation become receptacles. To escape a dangerous fate, they must destroy the receptacle or break the Soissons vase, as Clovis did. Fragment the idols, the golden calf, but also Moses' Tables. The saviour is an idol. Shattering idols makes it possible to restrain the feeling of omnipotence linked to the desire for eternity. Nothing is eternal and nothing is immutable. To break is to transform, to go from one form to another. Moses breaks the Tables of the Law to make a note of the Hebrews' sin. God then gives back the Tables of the Law and he recomposes them. That is what "recognizing imperfection" means. God becomes able to reconstitute the Tables. There we have a lovely metaphor for Transformation, thanks to the following pattern: a non-immutable form, a regression comes in, a form that breaks, the creation of another form. Both regressions (the sin of Israel, the destruction of the Tables of the Law) are, therefore, legitimate insofar as they are useful; they cannot be avoided, but they must be overcome and one must understand their reasons. When both temples in Jerusalem and the walls of Jericho are destroyed twice within the space of over three thousand years, we again have the destruction, punctually, of the paralyzing receptacle that prevents the pursuing of the travel of Transformation.

What, in that context, is the role of the consultant?

His role is primarily about enabling the leader or the co-author of Transformation to understand that he is, first of all, a receptacle. The consultant, therefore, accompanies the co-author of transformation in this shattering of the receptacle, through working on the resistances in particular. He also has to understand what the collusions between the co-author of transformation and the external projections are that he is receiving. Let us imagine a vase put under pressure coming as much from the outside as from the inside, a vase with wheels, mobile on the road to Transformation. Opposite forces will cancel each other out, until paralysis is reached, until the effect of those too strong pressures leads the receptacle to explode. Projections (external) and introjections (internal) converge on the brims of the vase, thereby blocking any movement along the road to Transformation. The role of the consultant is to help process both projections and introjections, by transforming the space and the receptacle's surface-boundaries, thereby making the receptacle disappear rather than accepting its explosion. My role, to get back to the alternative that we started from, is to transform the receptacle into a container, and thus to give back the flow and the freedom of movement.

This is the same metaphor as the one about the river bank and the embankment. Putting the projections back into the flow of Transformation whilst not allowing them to stop it . . .

I think that the biblical deluge is also a way of putting movement back into a blocked, annihilated mankind. God provoked a deluge to put the flow back in movement, at the risk of total destruction, maybe. However, by creating Noah's Ark, a new progression is made possible following the regression that the deluge represents. The story of Jonah and the whale enables, in a similar way, to "save" a man, in other words Man, swallowed up by the whale to enable him to do part of the journey of Transformation hidden and protected in the "black box".

In Collodi's The Adventure of Pinocchio, *the puppet is also at one point swallowed up by a whale. He too is a real metaphor for transformation from the state of inanimate puppet, from a piece of wood, to one of a child, to a human being.*

Indeed, I hadn't thought of it. I would like to add that the consultant's purpose is also to protect, by hiding him, part of the leader's or his co-authors' journey of Transformation. He does so by attracting onto himself some of the projections. The difference between leaders, managers, co-authors, and the consultant is that the latter is paid for that, for the work that is foreseeable and anticipated in the here and now, which he does on his own or with his colleagues. Therefore, and this is not a marginal issue, a consultant needs a team.

This risk that the consultant runs, by attracting towards him some of the projections, which as we've seen can be very destructive, is at a high cost, I imagine. Do you get paid a lot of money for your interventions?

I get paid more or less money depending on the cases. A consultant is a professional of the transformation of projections. Consequently, he or she gets good money for their capacity to elaborate transference. When he or she gets paid, they have to get good money, because working precisely with projections is very dangerous and a consultant is not omnipotent. The same goes for professional soldiers or technical operators in a nuclear power station. Remuneration isn't solely of a financial dimension. It is also the fruit of an acknowledgement process. Consultants are not marquis or courtiers, they are more like knights and they see themselves, as much as possible, as being free. They are not necessarily creators, but they are more like reproducers. Being a consultant is very much a growing profession and it is probably useful to explain my approach. A consultant's duty is first of all to work on the "why" and not on the "how". In that way they offer a support for the navigation, but they are not the ones navigating.

They are members external to the crew, they don't belong to the ship but they do help to interpret the elements that influence navigation. A consultant is a hermeneutist (see Hermes or Mercury) and an interpreter. He works through the heuristic. A consultant is not an external observer and his history resembles that of the anthropologists'. In the beginning they operated as external observers, then—thanks to Malinovski and to Levi-Brulle—they realized two things: first of all the simple fact of observing modifies the situation that you are observing; then the only way of understanding is to understand through internalizing. One must run the risk of letting oneself be "invaded", of losing one's own identity. The risk in the case of a consultant is of becoming a pseudo-manager. For me, the only way to know and to understand is through the body itself, from head to toes. In fact, you have to immerse yourself in the liquid of the institution in transformation and accept to be, first of all, the recipient then become, in part, the container. It is like floating on your back in the sea, or as the Italian language conveys it so symbolically: *fare il morto* (pretending to be dead). This is why, borrowing from the language of psychoanalysis, we can speak of a "floating ear". Floating on your back or pretending to be dead is in fact accepting to be in contact with death, with the institution's entropy. It is not about behaving as if, but about really connecting with Thanatos. Finally, the consultant's listening ear relates to a diffuse attention, because it is impossible to maintain a vigilant presence all the time, and anyway it serves no real purpose!

What you are saying reminds me of a metaphor about attention derived from Elemire Zolla's study, when in one of his books he talks about the Navy officers' gaze "lost" on the horizon: a unique gaze that enables them to locate a submarine, in the distance, at water level. A gaze that I would qualify as a "floating" one.

The description is right and interesting, but a consultant is not a radar nor a sonar, and he is even less the officer on the lookout. The consultant is the one who interprets the signals. Just as he is not a computerized technician but a human being, he must equally and imperatively interpret internal signals. His intimate resonances come from the received projections.

Do you have an example?

In a very prosaic way, needing to urinate during an intervention is a signal as much as the frequency with which this need comes back! But premonitions and intuitions are also signals. We surround them with some kind of magical halo because we don't understand that they come from a work, both conscious and unconscious, and from a situation that produces signs. Noises and signs that, most of the time, we neglect. Intuition is the fruit, not of a lack of preparation, as many seem to think, but well and truly from previous harsh work that makes possible the internalization of the flow of freedom. This goes, for example, for our meeting: it had nothing to do with miracle ... It is the consequence of both our work and of our mutual propensity for Transformation. The same can be said of so-called premonitions. In another way, a consultant is a provocateur, which, etymologically, opens new ways and gives a new voice for words to be spoken. There is a multiplicity of voices, a polyphony that, in the vast majority of cases, becomes mute by fear of complexity. The consultant's duty, with members of the institution, is to make appear—by provoking them—some of these voices which constitute, in the "here and now", new resources for the transformation of the institution. A consultant can, for example, accompany the birth of words newly spoken in those sub-systems in the institution that are usually the most silent. But certain brakes must regulate the releasing of new voices or else a real danger can appear. It is not about giving rise to the damned of the Earth that the International talks about, but about enabling the silent ones to talk.

A consultant is also a frontier runner, someone who accompanies the migration, very rarely in the role of the leader, rather in the one of clarifier, of socio-psychic (as opposed to medico-psychiatric) agent. Indeed, a consultant facilitates the alternation of sedentary and nomadic states that characterize each journey of Transformation. Because travelling doesn't imply constant movement, it involves a succession of regressions, progressions, and breaks, be they physical or psychic, political or spiritual. In most travels, you set up camp for the night. The journey of Transformation is not atavism but it is distinct and reflected upon action. In the case of the cancer treatment centre when we decided to leave, it was of course out of fear, but also out of discernment. The chock of revelation, which shows up the mortifying and self-punishing management, was of such violence, of such disturbance, that it appeared necessary for us to have a break. To use the title of a cowboy movie, "When the heat rises in El Paso", one must remain cautious, have a break, so that El Paso does not become El Pazzo![1]

You are alluding, between those lines, to the leadership of the consultant. What can he do to protect himself from the temptation of becoming an actual leader?

A consultant is a leader of interpretation, the client is a leader of action. In terms of ontology rather than in terms of deontology, one of the most definite crimes that a consultant can commit is to substitute himself for the manager of the institution, by feeding into the fusion and the confusion, in other words into the madness. From a practical point of view, the consultant is not responsible for the manager's decisions: the most he can be asked is to terminate the contract. The manager, conversely, will in any case have to live with the consequences of the intervention. In fact a consultant does not give advice in terms of decisions and of actions, so that to define him in terms of adviser is misleading. A consultant does not get paid to give advice, but to help contain the projections; he gets paid to work on the conditions of the decision-making, bringing clarifications and elements that are different and other. In that regard, a consultant is an obstetrician or a midwife, which resonates with the origin of "maieutic". A consultant does not give advice but he does lend himself as a person, as a surface for projections, and as a workshop for interpreting the hidden things, to use the title of a book by Rene Girard. It is essential for him to live with the modesty and the humility that are brought about by the respect owed to those who form the institution, the very people with whom he is working. We consultants are humble frontier runners; humility must be understood in its etymological sense of humus and the fertile earth. Humility makes it possible to be in touch with the glebe, to have your feet on and in the ground. Did you know that in Hebrew, glebe is one of the origins of Adam? Adam means the man made of glebe, the glebus, as Chouraqui proved it. This is why a consultant is, first of all, a human being with his imperfections, his desire, his anxiety, and his freedom. A historical reference to the consultant is the honest man of the seventeenth century. He is a cultivated man with moral integrity who today is incarnated by a man who understands and acts in the world.

Of course, consultant and manager (including a manager in terms of one who governs his own freedom) meet on the joint field of discernment and we can talk here about complementary leadership. The world of consultants is the world of working hypotheses, whereas the world of managers is the world of working the hypotheses. A working hypothesis is only useful if it enables action, decision, and consequently transformation, or Trans-Form-Action. If, for example, by intervening in an institution, I highlight the hypothesis of "dependency" from which it suffers, I don't do it for the pleasure of the intellectual discovery, but so that the institution can benefit from the advantages of the progressive journey towards interdependency.

If I highlight a hypothesis of an overwhelming feeling of guilt in a system, I do it so that that system can free itself and acquire some responsibility, and more to the point so that there can be a decrease in self-punishment and a move towards self-promotion; which is equivalent to putting the system back in motion with the help of working hypotheses that become instruments of transformation.

Equally, being alone is another point that links consultant and leader, and in fact every human being. If what characterizes a manager is being alone, he will find himself in extreme loneliness at certain times during his decision-makings. This happens when he makes his choices of investments, redundancies, alliances, colleagues or successor. In each of these choices, the manager is alone. The people around him in the organization, even those endowed with the greatest honesty and the best lucidity, are in a relationship of dependency towards the manager, a dependency that can be processed to a greater or lesser extent. The consultant won't be there to cancel out this manager's loneliness, which is co-substantial to his role. However, he is there to enable the manager to work with the loneliness, to transform it, and at the same time to avoid that loneliness becoming isolation. Isolation can remove a manager from reality. It comes from projections and introjections and feeds omnipotence and, therefore, impotence and fantasies of omniscience. In other words he will end up losing consciousness.

In what ways can a consultant work "on" the manager's or the leader's loneliness?

The way in which a consultant is in resonance with the manager's loneliness becomes a means of recognizing, elaborating, and transforming this loneliness. The loneliness of the one who produces decisions corresponds to the loneliness of the one who produces interpretations. I am referring to the loneliness suggested by Gabriel Garcia Marquez, the author of *Hundred Years of Solitude*: "Solitude is the isolation of interpretations." In fact, the capacity to make interpretations shortens the distance between self and others, hence the true origin of the word: inter-pretation. Interpreting connects people, without cancelling out the loneliness, and by elaborating it precisely in the relationship with others. Conversely, isolation is entropic and mortifying. The sharing of loneliness thereby prevents the establishing of isolation. The dialectical relationship between the leader's loneliness and that of the consultant is undoubtedly the best protection against the propagation of the destructive fires of isolation. It stems from my proposition of a shared management, which bears witness, in effect, to the sharing of each leader's loneliness. And here we find again the ontological necessity for the existence of the other. Our own loneliness is not exceptional, because it is the individual lot of everyone. I am talking about the humanity of loneliness, and not, of course, of the presumed heroism of solitude. Loneliness is not a spectacle, it is an act; it is not a melodrama, it is drama; it is not some representation, it is tragedy. Solitude becomes dangerous when it is portrayed as heroic. Every human being carries the baggage of loneliness, but this burden is heavier for some than for others. For example, leaders (from the heads of the government to the managers) sometimes make decisions that have vital consequences for a great number of people. The loneliness thus needs to be shared, even if such a sharing cannot cancel it out. The sharing enables an encounter between individuals and generates, in that way, identity. It is a vicious circle—loneliness, sharing, encounter, and identity—that could conceivably "unveil" the mystery of human existence, a mystery that constitutes precisely the indestructible part of what we have called the black box. This vicious circle can, nevertheless, make it possible to reduce the volume of this black box. It makes it possible, in the here and now, to dispose of the glass box that creates isolation through transparent walls: physical, but mostly psychic and spiritual isolation. This can also be conveyed to us by Marcel Marceau's famous miming act in which he tries in vain to get out of a box that keeps closing down ever more on him. The vicious circle, described above, carries with it, in addition, the role of container (and not of receptacle), a container that makes it possible to *cum-tenere*, to process, to share the projections and therefore to conceive an open system.

An open system allows containment, whereas a closed system brings compression and finally explosion; such is the paradox. I think that a most striking example is that of states that exchange men, cultures and merchandises with each other through their borders and of those who, in contrast, take position in their own "limes", which is precisely a … frontier.

I thoroughly agree and talking about us, I would say that today our relationship has come across as being, at least in part, an open system under construction and elaboration, given its capacity to transform negative projections that have at last taken shape, that of "your" dragon.

*   *   *

The notes that "annotate" the ten days of interview with David Gutmann were not written "live". Today, for example, is a day in March and not in August. And I am not in Ostuni, but in Bari. Opposite the window in my apartment, to which I moved only a few weeks ago, there is a psychiatric asylum. One of the patients is singing a Bob Marley tune at the top of his voice, behind the bars on his windows, on the top floor. In the silence of morning's first few hours, in the surrounding street, a vigorous, painful complaint is also tainted with a strange and involuntary cheerfulness. If the man weren't singing, he would be confined anyway, and maybe even worse. Perhaps this chant is the relic, I would almost like to say "the nostalgia", if that word wasn't so literal, of his freedom and his health. What can his story be? Was he really mad or was he simply an unsettled man removed from the world as has happened to so many others? Asylums for lunatics: I wonder if those who work there have ever given thought to the idea of psychic containment? Have they limited themselves to being only a receptacle for madness? Receptacles that explode periodically, to the point that everyone now in Italy—including the law—is asking for their closure (although only a few actually ask themselves what container could replace them effectively).

I think of the ephemeral boundaries between illness and well-being in an institution. Before getting to the desperate chant, there will be dramatic squeaks, wrong notes, background noises that signal the need to put back into motion the flow of identity. I think of the work of elaboration that alone allows a constructive action. I think of the luminous pages written by a very lucid and "concerned" sociologist, Eglio Resta, in his new book Le Stele e le Masserizie, *which already, through its title, refuses the omnipotent delirium of the man who—as we can read in the* Dialogue between a Goblin and a Gnome *(1824)—even wants to acquire the stars for his own furniture, giving up desire, which by definition is "sidereal", nostalgic for the stars. Resta writes: "journeys, first of all, those of identity, indicate trajectories, movements, a way of proceeding for sure but defined by the movement itself. And in plural: they are numerous, they are all different, they can be cyclical, sagittal, interrupted, but all together and each time journeys." David would say: "with zigzags". Later Resta notes that Freud had been astonished by the method of an Italian doctor, Giovanni Morelli, who could identify a work of art through some clue, some detail, some trace. Just like Michelangelo's Moses, about which Freud wrote a famous essay in 1914, "through the detail of a finger that interrupts the movement of the beard, he can be reconstructed differently from what is consigned by the biblical tradition: he did not throw, irascible, the tables of the law but contained the drive", reminds the sociologist.*

From last summer to today, I have surprised myself to discover how David's working hypotheses remind me of the ones of authors that I value. It is certainly the case with Eligio Resta, who at one point in the book, claims, "institutions remember and forget in exactly the same way as individuals do." And the philosopher Salvatore Natoli, alludes to the biblical scholar Sergio Quinzio, the apocalyptic Christian who magnificently researched the Hebraic roots of modernity. Natoli writes: "modernity insofar as it has been a metamorphosis of the Judaeo–Christian tradition, took seriously the idea of transformation seen as a praxis."

It is the case with the Ligurian writer, Francesco Biamonti, who on the "high lands" of the border with France, contemplates his existence modelled on the "frontier runners", on the smugglers of things and tongues (and silences) and on a hermeneutic of beauty. Again I think of Hermes, Mercury, the messenger with winged-sandals, god of language, meditation, and interpretation.

I have in my room a framed parchment, dated 24th March 1961. I was eighteen months old. It is an acrostic that was given to me by my paternal grandfather and it warns that I, his grandson, am protected by the God, Mercury. From the house across the road no chanting can be heard any more. I feel that Mercury is necessary to keep sane.

Note

1. In the Italian text, "*El Pazzo*" means "The Madman".

CHAPTER EIGHT

Here and now, or the flavour of experience

We were talking yesterday of *container* and *receptacle*. To better understand, one must take into consideration not only the shattering of the receptacle, but also its possible overflowing. In fact the intensity and the multiplicity of projections can trigger an explosion or an overflow, a burst in the river bank or the river actually spilling over the embankment. Even river banks—since miracles and omnipotence do not exist—can be swallowed up by the water. When a phenomenon of massive and totalitarian projections is happening, it is often already too late. The work of transforming projections must be started much earlier. The transformation of projections is a constant *praxis* with more or less intense phases. If one decides to call it *prevention*, it becomes a practice by experience. A certain action can sometimes be useful. The setting up of *Blockers* in a situation, for example in the case of Wall Street, can "raise the river banks" to the maximum limit. However, in an institution prevention means calling in a real consultant, creating a role of observer and designing indicators, such as the percentage of turnover or of work related accidents. It involves organizing meetings for "discernment" and, even when the crisis is mortifying, preparing crisis cells which can only really be useful after the discernment phase. However, and I will say it again, one must accept that, when a massive and invasive process of destructive projections is at work, even the most efficient of containers may not work. What is needed is then to preserve, rather than to save, the capacity for containment, so that it can get back into action after a while. Thus, escaping or taking one's distances can become an act of lucidity and courage, as it was in the case of Mao Ze Tung's Long March. The Yi King and Sun Tzu's *The Art of War* actually advise it. Digestion is another metaphor for Transformation. During digestion, it becomes necessary to have a break, to stop feeding oneself and, in case of difficulties, to take natural or synthetic medication. Excesses are inevitable in Transformation and it is then about recognizing them so that they do not become irreparable. The "accepted" retreat is part of a kind of management of regression, as did the Russians with Napoleon and Hitler, to better defeat them later on. By the way, do you know this Jewish joke? "What was the Soviet experts' advice to the Egyptians during the Six-Day War? Retreat and wait for winter"! The here and now had been forgotten. Fidel Castro in the Cuban sierra, the Viet-Kongs fighting the French or the Americans, or conversely the Russians in Afghanistan and in Chechnya, all retreated. It was not by chance that the one who negotiated with the Chechnyans was General Lebed. He had already tasted defeat in Afghanistan. This illustrates of the coupling of the affects *Courage* and *Fear*. Fear is something that is indispensable and to accept it relieves feelings of guilt. Fear is a good advisor in some situations and in others it isn't. Only discernment makes it possible to understand which is which. There are no heroes, there is no omnipotence that hold: it is legitimate to be afraid. If the hero is Zorro, then I would say that it rhymes with Zero.

You spoke about experience. For you, who set up your own company and called it "Praxis International", is experience, in other words practice, definitely more important than any kind of theory …

In the concept of experience, you have practice, necessity for the other, and use. Nothing can replace practice. Trainers (in French *formateurs*) are in fact transformers (in French *trans-formateurs*). They accompany the passage not of knowledge, but of practice. The latter creates knowledge and, therefore, the interpretation of life through partial and temporary working hypotheses of the here and now. Galileo wrote, "it is not possible to teach others anything. One can only help them discover it." Nothing can replace the use and the practice, but on their own, they are not enough. Practice without interpretation leads to repetition. Hence, the necessity for the other. A trainer is in fact a transformer who enables each individual to forge his or her own experience, comprehension, and interpretation. However, as is shown in *cum-prendere* and in *inter-pretare*, this can only be achieved within a relationship with others. We can see the connection, through the Latin roots of words, to the essential imperative of the other! The dialectical relationship with the other facilitates the forging of one's own experience, but more importantly of one's own identity. *Consultancy* and necessity for the other are already intimately linked in their etymology, which points to the evolution of the function of consultancy and of the role of consultant. In the beginning came the oracle, the unique and totalitarian answer. Then, we had the formulation of the question in terms that make possible the intervention of a consultant and of the members of the institution. Consulting means asking for advice, consultancy is plural deliberation. It is, therefore, beneficial in the struggle against the idea of a saviour and the idea of omnipotence. Consultants have a duty to have colleagues or referents, and can only be in strong mutual resonance with the members of the institution. Even though, sadly, a consultant is often perceived as an oracle.

Particularly when you think that in Italy a group of researchers writes an annual report called … "Delphi"!

In the oracle there is prediction, prayer, and also an answer from the gods. But what we really need is questions from men.

Why is it that, beyond their origin, consultancy and the need for the other are so closely linked?

Because a consultant in an institution can be considered as the symbol or the archetype of the other. Also, because everyone has the capacity to become their own consultant, what I call *consultant in the mind*. The role of an external consultant is, therefore, to develop simultaneously the internal, endogenous, and internalized potential for consultancy, both in each of the members of the institution and in the institution as a system. Consultancy is not only for the professional consultant. From my experience, I can say that the best managers are those who can develop a disposition for consulting to their life, to their institution, and to the development of that institution. More technically speaking, the role of a manager necessarily includes a sub-role of consultant. This phenomenon doesn't affect the necessity for external and professional consultancy; on the contrary, when a manager makes use of his own capacities for consultancy, the dialogue becomes richer, more complex, more demanding, and more productive. Through mirroring, each has the capacity to develop his potential for management, which I call *the management in the mind*, firstly for himself and then for the institution in which he works. This is a fundamental reason why a consultant should get about his activity in the context of a consultancy firm or in close relationship with one: it is only in that way that he will manage to acquire an experience of institutional life and, therefore, of the management of daily life.

More generally, the institutional dimension of a consultant can lead him to connect directly with the role of manager. In my case, the fact that I created a commercial consultancy firm and that I am its president, clearly made it possible for me, after seven or eight years, to better understand my clients' problems. Furthermore, in this case, being a manager enables one to resist the professional bias of the *consultant in the mind*, the temptation to always be in a position of interpretation and of offering working hypotheses. To be manager of oneself, then, becomes an exercise of humility. It is about having one's feet in the humus, in the fertile glebe. Would you allow me, however, to come back to the etymological roots of *experience*, which offer us a decisive and crucial understanding? *Experience* comes from the Greek *empeiria* which means "to undertake a travel" and from the Latin *ex-perior, experientia* which means "to go through the difficulties of a trial, of an ordeal", where *ex* links back to "the mean to" and *perentia* alludes to *periculum*. Therefore, experience is, in fact, an ordeal through which one acquires or learns something, by getting out of the danger on the path that is becoming too narrow. In this definition, there is a link

back to the notion of travel, of journey, of path, of passage, which
are at the heart of the Transformation-Approach. What the
etymology of experience brings is the idea that the path of our
life, without a process of transformation, has a tendency to become
narrower and to bring us to a cul-de-sac, in an impasse that not only
is blocking us, but also paralyses us and sterilizes us. I am currently
reading *Assassins*, a "detective" story by Philippe Djian, author of
the novel from which the film *Betty Blue* was made. This morning I
found, on page 116, this sentence referring to the female character, it
struck me and I would like to convey it: ". . . She started to leave the
road she was travelling on, and to take a path that was becoming
narrower and narrower, and she got lost after going round in
circles". The quote enlightens us in a very practical way, that not
only does the path of life become narrower, but there is also a
tendency to go round in circles, just like a prisoner in his cell. The
Transformation-Approach makes it possible, through the practice of
zigzagging, to avoid going round in circles, without falling headfirst
into the omnipotent phantasy of life as a straight line. This is how
one can get out of a mortifying circle. Only experience can, on the
one hand, teach us to contain the anxiety of the zigzags, and to steer
ourselves, following the unavoidable narrowing, towards a con-
tinuation and a stretching out of the path. Only experience can tell
us that the ford of Transformation can be crossed and does not have
to feel like an insurmountable obstacle. Experience is the only way
of becoming involved, without premature impasse, in a process of
transformation by accepting its inevitable term, that is death.
Learning from experience does not exclude other forms of learning,
for example didactic forms of learning, which are necessary at
certain stages of life (a child who learns to read and write: a learning
that Piaget, in fact, demonstrated was founded on some experiential
basis). However, if experimental or rather "experiential" learning is
stopped, other types of learning will soon become useless. In fact, a
father and a mother, a teacher, a trainer, a consultant can pass on
specific, familiar pieces of knowledge, but they will never be able to
pass on their own experience. The role of *trans-formers*,[1] their true
role, is undoubtedly to clarify the importance of the learning process
in its non-transmissible aspect more than in its contents. Experience
cannot be passed on, but its taste can. Only the desire for experience
can be aroused. Between too habitual a practice, which turns our life

into an impasse (after having spent a long time going round in circles), and the phantasy, comparable to a motorway layout that claims to guide our existence, only Transformation, with its zigzags, makes it possible for us to develop simultaneously both the journey and the journeying.

When you talk about "motorway", are you referring to the idea or the myth of Progress?

For me Progress doesn't exist, only Transformation does, made up of progressions and regressions. Progress is a fantasy myth, an object of desire. Progress is both a project and an object, whereas progression is both a journey and a subject. It can exist only in relation to regression, just as construction only exists in relation to destruction. I feel myself to be a Jew from the Diaspora, of Ashkenazi origin and whose parents survived the genocide. I belong to the first French generation, which maybe returned to France after many centuries. Even though I was born in France, I was naturalized by decree at the age of four, before that I guess I was stateless. Come to think of it, I am the result of a journey and of a transfer, firstly in the geographical meaning of the word. My whole life, therefore, consists in not being the passive object of transference, but in contrast, in becoming an active subject of Transformation. This led me to psychoanalysis. I am not a survivor or Alain Finkielkraut's *Imaginary Jew*. I have refused, first of all unconsciously and then more and more consciously, the confusion between being a survivor and being the son of a survivor. I can feel, deep within me, my existence as *living* and not *surviving*,[2] inheriting a personal, family, and community history and inheriting a Hebraic tradition. But I have also inherited another tradition, that of my country, France, in a Europe that is Greek, Latin, catholic, protestant, Christian. My way of being a living being is not to make a synthesis, but to enable the different elements of what we are talking about to reason and more importantly to resonate within me. I use what is specific to each of them, but also what they have in common. This practice of resonance has also led me to make use of other traditions: Asiatic, especially Chinese and Japanese, but also African and Arab. I draw on the Hebraic tradition for the endless questioning about identity and the relationship with others, the opening based on the uniqueness of each of us. The Hebraic experience can be considered as a permanent archetype, between the spiritual, the psychic, and the political, sometimes banal, too often tragic. What can you say, what can you do, in relation to the ephemeral, the futility of every existence? This question, present in each of us, is symbolized by the Jewish experience. But I don't mean to say that the Hebraic condition is an illustration of the human condition, of Robert Antelme's *human species*, which would mean that we are alive, subject only to certain conditions. The Transformation-Approach was born from a Hebraic tradition, but it has developed through facing other traditions, western and eastern. Also, the fact of *carrying* forward this approach is not accidental. It is not by chance and probably comes from my specific existential experience. When someone, as it happened to me, is the object of a psychic and physical *transfer*, whether it is through projections on Jews or geographical migrations, there are very few alternatives. He either flees into madness, atavism, or the accumulation of money or he confronts issues face to face by interpretation and the discovery for self and for others. Which, by the way, explains the noticeable number of Jewish doctors, lawyers, musicians, and physicists. *Understanding Transformation makes it possible to live, and not to survive*: I formulated it in this way, but this declaration is too neat to be honest. Things are not black and white. I am not describing a result, but a journey that comes from a desire that is ambivalent given its very nature. I am not describing a realization; rather I am expressing my relationship to an absence. *Desire can only exist through lack*, writes Lacan. But Lacan may be a bit too intellectualist in this case. I am talking about a real lack: that of my grandparents, uncles, and cousins. I am talking about the collective lack of the six million dead in the Shoah. I am talking about the lack of my roots, which only get expressed through my parents and a few Jewish friends. I am talking about the disappearance of a link to my history. I am also talking about a grief that was, for many years, impossible for my parents, my sister, my brother, and myself, to talk about, in particular, the mourning of my father's first children, our *half brothers and sister*. I am talking about the near impossibility to be in mourning, *vis-à-vis* those beings that I do not know. This mourning that destroys survivors and their children. The experience of Transformation, which intervened with all its conceptualizations, does not seek to, nor can it, save everyone, but it allows us to live our life in the *here and now*. This condition, this experience, this praxis of the extreme which I wish upon no one, can only be dissolved by Transformation; and this through drawing on the different traditions and, in particular, on the Hebraic tradition of interpretation.

I have been able to elaborate on my professional and personal experience to give birth to this synthesis, or rather this fully human hybrid that the Transformation-Approach represents. Why was it me, and not someone else, who was able to partially develop this approach? I do not know. This is part of the *black box*. But I know that I was finally able to process the grief of my *half-brothers and sister*, of my father's first wife, and of six million Jewish dead. It is a process of individualization, an inductive and deductive march. It is finding one's own life. I was a child shaken about in the course of the involuntary, imposed, collective journey of survivors that was a mortifying journey. In contrast, I fight today to be the author of my own journey, in other words co-author. I have come out of the journey of a horde. My birth is the result of the action of two hordes: the Nazi horde, who wanted to reduce Jews, gypsies, homosexuals, and communists to their state of horde to be exploited and exterminated. To overcome and transform this state, the work of survivors comes in, and of their children helped in the context of a return to the state of civilization, including the *individuation* of every person that Jung talks about. The potentiality to be a desiring individual and the capacity to be *with* is civilization. It is about not being an aberration or a clone any more—I have been that—and to become an exception just like every other human being. Living and not surviving, it is not even reliving. Living is simply living here and now, *without memory or desire*—as Bion would remind us. It is having the capacity to be in the moment, internalizing others, the other, those who are alive and those who are dead and those who will follow. We are at the opposite end to omnipotence and omniscience, whilst at the same time respecting the fact that everyone is the melting pot of humankind. On the psychic and spiritual dimensions, I do not want to be the representative of anyone. I want to be myself with my own internalizations. Others are in me, such as my *half-brothers and sister*, but I do not represent them. Have you ever thought why North-American cinema has so many Jewish producers and directors? With their films, they address six hundred million people in relation also to six million deceased Jews. When so many of a community's beings have been exterminated, those who are left, and their descendants, then use means of communication that are likely to touch the greatest number of people. I do not speak in the name of others, but I speak with the others in me. Transformation allows for those human beings in me to be pacified and not bellicose, or at least more pacified than bellicose, in order to push my creativity to be more creative than inhibited. The I is I, it is never we. However, the I can only be such, through internalizing the others.

*   *   *

I am thinking of the individual and the group. The whole twentieth century is interspersed, tormented, lacerated by this antinomy of modernity. It would be presumptuous to talk about it here, in one small page of this "diary of Transformation". To the "we", at the entering of the masses in history we owe the redeeming of the silence, of the misery, but also of the horror, the tragedy of the "brief century". Masses and power intimately linked in a pact of death, according to Canetti. On an other hand, what long road does the "I" still have to pursue, to finally feel himself full, mortal, and different to others? Others with whom he has to cohabitate! The century is ending with the millenary and pushes us into a "group" angst, an anxiety of gnosticism, of cheap and minimal ideologies. It takes us into dimensions that "rescue" individuals, welcome them into a maternal bosom, take them out of history, restore them, infantilize them, deceive them. "To not condemn, to not approve: to understand"—such is Spinoza's persistent warning. But who will understand the "I" when he is surrounded by the groups, annihilated by the masses and ruined in a war that isn't his? So much violence, still, more than half a century after Auschwitz, for example in a Europe where being Croat or Serb or Muslim has become, out of the blue, more important than to love the eyes of the young girl at the window across the street, where "belonging" suddenly counts infinitely more than "being"? What madness hides behind the scientific rejoicings of the ever more concrete possibility of cloning man? The eternally "same" is the reproducible and the perfect(!) Frankenstein is a modern Prometheus crazy about technology. In the dream, the nightmare of the clone resides, in its entirety, the drifting of the mass, whereas what we need is the different, the unique, the imperfect as the fragile and courageous "I"s.

Notes

1. See p. 104 for the use of the dual meaning of *trans-formateurs* in French.
2. In French, *vivant et non pas survivant*.

CHAPTER NINE

Black box and glass box

*W*e were saying yesterday that to recognize one's own is to recognize tradition in general and thus to open oneself to other traditions.

It is exactly the opposite of uniformity. A uniformity that transpires, for example, in this Coca-Cola advert in which young people from different countries in the world all drink this beverage with their traditional dish. Tradition is also part of what I define as the *black box*, this part of us that is incompressible and incomprehensible. It is the unconscious, and we can only reduce its volume up to a certain limit and only temporarily.

The zigzags coming out of the *black box* are comparable to the emerged part of an iceberg. You can't photograph the *black box*. At the most you could film it, because it is in perpetual motion. It accompanies the travel of Transformation, it moves along the journey, stage after stage. Reducing its volume is a continuous attempt. It is the barrel of the Danaides, an endless labour. You have there a beautiful metaphor for freedom, which is a discontinuous flow. There is, for me, a very strong link between the incomprehension of the *black box* and freedom. We can't know everything, and it is only in that way that we are imperfectly free.

You also talk in your writings of a "glass box". What is it about, could we summarize it?

The *glass or transparent box* is perhaps the box of the preconscious. We see it whilst at the same time we don't. This concept was born in 1993, three years after the one about the black box, after a personal trauma and crisis. Things are there, the elements are visible, comprehensible and not hidden, but we don't see them. Why? It's because we don't want to see them. Seeing them would force us to act.

Can you give us an example?

My wife betrays me, I have all the elements to realize it, but I pretend nothing is happening. Because to make a note of it would oblige me to act.

It is an "acte manqué"?[1]

An *acte manqué* is in effect a successful act! It is an *acting out*. Here, in contrast, there is no action.

Does the same go for organizations?

Certainly. In organizations the glass box is very developed and very heavy.

For example, in an extremely conflicted company, one of the leaders, my client, tells me that he is experiencing a real success in not being attacked by his colleagues any more. My answer to him was "this is not a transformation any more, but a miracle! Your colleagues are, in reality, preparing a massive attack against you, in secret. Precisely because you have become fortunate in business, the usual attacks have become inefficient, which implies that you have become stronger. The envy towards you has not diminished but has increased. There is therefore a collusion at work to prepare an offensive that will surprise you." And that was exactly what happened.

The facts are there, but we don't see them because it is tiring to be attentive all the time. On the subject of the black box, I would like to add something on cancer. Cancer is an uncontrolled chain reaction. The reality that we can contrast it with is sexual reproduction: the meeting of two different elements who give birth to a third element. In the case of an uncontrolled chain reaction, it leads only and quickly to death. In the case of sexual reproduction, the reaction leads to life and, therefore, to death. Thus, entropy pushes away and attempts to exclude the encounter, the interpretation, the Big Bang, by asserting that the two parties are *a priori* incompatible. Just like racism.

And what are the consequences?

The consequence is to try to suppress one of the two parties, the other, so as to suppress the fear, the anxiety and the freedom that exist in all institutions but are alive and in transformation. From that perspective, for example, the popularity of a concept like *consensus* is a production of entropy.

In what way? Is consensus not actually the basis for democracy?

Maybe, but life is not consensual, it is in conflict. It is out of the confrontation coming from conflict that a new stage in the Transformation process can emerge. The opposite of *consensus* is not *disagreement* but *conflict*. We are linking back here to the Marxist approach: from the work on contradictions a creation can emerge. Occulting contradictions and conflicts is likely to be useful in the short-term, but in the long run those contradictions and those conflicts will erupt with a much stronger violence and destructive character. Thus, it is by far preferable to recognize these conflicts in order to understand them by analyzing the different elements at stake. The aim is to overcome and, therefore, transform them. Contradictions, conflicts, and oppositions thus become sources of Transformation, sources and resources for the construction of freedom and democracy. A consensual democracy, and I am now answering your question, runs the risk of preparing a bed for dictatorship. A process of containment, of contention, is once again necessary, whereas conversely the search for agreement is at all cost a sign of compression. The aim for consensus becomes fundamental, an end in itself, whereas consensus is a mean, which with other tools, forms part, at certain moments, of the journey of Transformation. This mean can become a stage in the journey, and the temptation is then to stop the journey at that moment. What is, in fact, the difference between democracy and fascism? Fascism says: "my idea must be everyone's idea and must be known and accepted by all." Fascism is the refusal of the existence of the *black box*. In fact, to accept the *black box* is to refuse the Black Shirt. Not processing the mourning means, in fact, maintaining it within oneself throughout life. Accepting the *black box*, carrier but above all creator of the mystery of life, with its contradictions and its conflicts, tends to prevent the obscurity and the blackness from invading all of our life. In Western culture, black represents death, darkness, and the Unknown. In other cultures, it is exactly the opposite. In Japan white is the colour of death. The main thing is differentiation, including with colours. For me, Pierre Soulages is, with Tapies, the greatest contemporary painter. He works exclusively with black, but manages to create a range of colours that are extremely diverse, a bit like Le Titien. Soulages brings into play the relationship between black, matter, and light. Everyone sees his works differently, depending on the location of the exhibition and the surrounding light. Each of Soulages' paintings denotes an extraordinary diversity and opens the way for a multiplicity of interpretations. This is done with the utmost simplicity, in a sobriety, a *despoiling* which brings to my mind *Apulia*, the region where we are, whilst at the same time maintaining the greatest complexity, the greatest richness, a bit like Yves Klein and Alighiero Boetti. According to Freud, in a dream, a *displacement* follows a condensation. In linguistics, a *displacement* is a metonymy, whereas a *condensation* is a metaphor. For Freud, dreaming is real life touching the unconscious. Why are displacement and condensation linked? Because they make it possible to transport, into another space, a question or an issue that was blocked by resistances in the initial space. In the other space, the resistances disappear, or at least they have become weaker.

With regards to such a dynamic, what is the meaning of consultancy?

Finding and interpreting. Consultancy is, at the same time,

heuristic and hermeneutic. I sometimes say that a consultant is a gold digger who is sifting in the flow of a river. He starts with searching for the reef and then he sifts. The gold nuggets are such that they come out of the *black box*, they are its product. Often the sifter is not adapted and we are then dealing with the *glass box*.

May I ask a rather irreverent question? Are there not risks involved other than those concerning the "scatole",[2] risk of ... rompere le scatole? Which means, in less vulgar terms: is there not metaphorical excess that gets crystallized in the "boxes" against the anxiety of interpretation.

The Transformation-Approach can be considered as an epistemology of the relative and not of the absolute. Each epistemology has a totalitarian vocation in its willingness to completely explain the complexity of life and the world. The temptation would be great, for me or for the readers, to fall into that trap. If the Transformation-Approach claims to be too integrated, it will end up being "integriste".[3] We are not talking about categories, but about working hypotheses, by definition unfinished, and nevertheless able to generate other working hypotheses. In fact, the role of a working hypothesis is more broadly to produce thoughts and actions, and not only other hypotheses; in other words to be fertile. A working hypothesis, taken and accepted as such, is not a working hypothesis: it needs to be argued, corrected, contradicted. Its destiny is to die, either because it is off track or because it is *on* track enough to have an effect and to modify reality. It is a production of the *here and now*. The vocation of our book is to be criticized and extended and there we are linking back to the relationship with the other. My thinking was born in relation to the other; it can evolve only with the experience of the other, only if included in the relationship with the other. It is not about baptizing another religion, with a new church, a new Pope, new priests, a new dogma, and a new theology. For me, it is about bringing a new stone to the comprehension and to the acts of the human condition, without false modesty or futile vanity. I believe in what I am saying, I believe that it is useful in terms of individual and social *savoir-vivre*, but I also believe that it is a stage whose vocation is to be overtaken in the travel, whose very principle is to be prolonged by new stages.

What we have here is a tool for travelling, but it isn't the only one. It is a way of travelling that offers every human being the possibility of working towards creating their own mode of travel, including—I would hope—through seeking inspiration in the Transformation-Approach.

As a consultant, have you ever been involved, with your clients, in a competition in Transformation?

Competition yes, but not rivalry, the latter being, in contrast, fed by envy. I often end up saying: "you don't agree with me, fine, find something better"! Alternatives are a struggle against mediocrity. The metaphor of Gulliver is not only a metaphor about egalitarianism it is also precisely one about mediocrity, about soft consensus. Differences are not here to be reduced to the smallest common denominator, but to let us take advantage of the dialectic of the tensions that they generate (just like in an electrical transformer ...). Equally in genetics, the suppression of differences unleashes degenerative physical and psychic processes. Death to mediocrity! It represents and unleashes an irreversible regression and the temptation to suppress differences or to level things out downwards. The debate on normality, mediocrity or exceptionality, is for me the wrong debate. Every human being is exceptional, unique, and specific. He or she carries the seeds of a creation that is other, of a creation that never before has existed in that form. Depending on the circumstances, every group, every institution, every society, every system expresses a request for different managers and leaders. The so-called "average" citizen is a stupid category, created precisely to reassure or to justify the permanent occupation of power by "specialists". The problem, therefore, starts when the elite become permanent. For example, it seems clear to me that in Italy, the current political leaders—Prodi, Bossi, and Berlusconi—are the fruit of movements and discontinuities. To better explain myself, let us use the following diagram:

REPETITION	CREATION
REPRODUCTION	INNOVATION

My experience leads me to say that every human and social activity is influenced by these four driving principles. All four are necessary to life and its transformation. As we have already seen in the case of the affects, it is not a question of expressing any kind of value judgment, there is no good or bad. In every institution the four driving forces are at work and it is useful that they are. For example, the century of Enlightenment, rationalism, and Progress all claim to reject repetition and reproduction, in the same way as conservatives and reactionaries, *those who uphold Order*, have a tendency to reject anything that has to do with innovation and creation. Reality is not necessarily found at the centre of the diagram. The articulation of these four tendencies depends on the situation of the system within its environment. There is no *a priori* answer but, still in the Transformation-Approach, it is imperative to understand what happens in terms of interaction between the four tendencies, to be aware of the likely dysfunctions, and sometimes to make room for the necessary transformations. When one of the four driving principles excludes the others for any length of time, this unmistakably involves a regression, a "zag". One could say that *fanatical bureaucrats* are dominated by the repetition principle, *reasonable bureaucrats* by the reproduction principle, *reasonable entrepreneurs* by the creation principle, and *crazy entrepreneurs* by the "innovation" principle in its absolute form. The distinction is a bit of a caricature, rather categorical in its deformed or excessive view of reality, but it is well and truly real. There is no middle ground between these four principles. The fact of fighting against homeostasis helps us to understand the dominant driving principle at work in the *here and now*.

I think now is the opportunity to say what you mean by each of these principles, in order to understand their nature and how they work. Let's start with "Repetition".

Repetition is cloning: the fact of doing exactly the same thing every time, whatever the circumstances. In a company, it is necessary to have a certain amount of repetition, for example in the process of choosing investments, promotion by seniority, or in the way tax and NI forms are completed. In these cases, repetition does exist, but it is played out over a given period and we will call it *procedure or habit*. It gives a minimum security and a stable reference in the course of the travel of Transformation. Recognition signals that make possible the establishing of "boundaries" that don't have within them the danger of becoming LIMINES—irremovable barriers, where boundaries are typical of an open system, and "limits", of a closed system. The process of complaints and appeals is another example of salutary repetition. The justice system in a democracy carries within it, in its operations, an important, indispensable part of repetition. Montesquieu says it clearly in *The Spirit of Laws*.

"Reproduction"

Its most vivid metaphor is sexual reproduction. Of two systems who meet, in other words of the encounter with the other, a third system is born, which will include some of the characteristics of the genitor-systems, but also new ones. It is not a synthesis, but a hybrid. The difference may be infinitely minute, but it is difference. Management in companies must seek to support small modifications, adaptations, and evolutions that, without questioning the heart of processes and procedures, will manifest a taking into account of incitements and excitements. If we consider, for example, the choice of individuals in terms of recruitment or succession, then those who will be taken on will be those who are not clones, but who are well and truly the fruit of reproduction: mostly identical, but also different. Very often when we talk about *social reproduction*, in sociological terms, we mean, in fact, *social repetition*. *Social reproduction* is already a progression. Sadly, social mechanisms, in particular in the selection of elites, promote a social repetition out of a mimetic need—as Rene Girard writes—for fear of surprise and out of excessive anxiety. It is the logic of "long live immobilism!" both terms being somehow a little bit contradictory. In fact entropy, the death principle, *Thanatos*, leads to an overwhelming repetition and refuses, at the same time, reproduction. Cancer is nothing other than the transformation of differentiated cells into the multiplication of totally identical cells.

Let's move on to "Creation".

To create a new flesh, another body, another skin. This is a recurring theme in all the mythologies and all the cosmogonies. We talk about the creation of man through the transformation of another element. Adam was created from earth, through the glebe; Eve was created from Adam's rib. The creation of man is the symbol of transformation through the passage of form A to form B, which then becomes form C. Human beings always escape their creator. The result never matches the initial project. The form is never static nor immutable: it is always becoming—of course with some pauses—but always becoming. A is the earth, B would be Adam, who here doesn't allow himself to eat the apple. In contrast, C is Adam eating the forbidden apple and he is man of a journey and not man of a project. The very principle of creation is that the latter escapes its creator, which means that even God does not want himself omnipotent. In the first years of life, the creation is, first of all, a reproduction, a reproduction that is represented in the vital dependency towards the parents. But becoming an *inter*-dependent human being is really what matters: in other words, neither dependent, nor independent, but I shall say it again, interdependent. In a company, creation leads to simultaneously imagining both different services and new products, but also different processes, procedures, and systems to produce such goods and such services that are "other". Creation brings surprise, which is the best way of combating *emprise*, the forced appropriation. It is also interesting to note the Italian linguistic coincidence of *impresa*[4] and of *interpresa*,[5] as if the emprise–enterprise contained in its psycholinguistic genetic the very idea of imprisonment. *Emprise* is the hand of the past that pushes, in the worst cases, towards repetition and, in the best cases, towards reproduction. Pinocchio, Pygmalion, the Golem, Frankenstein (somebody said "the son of Einstein"!) are other metaphors for creation. Creation brings uncertainty, a dose of unknown in an institution and, if we understand the metaphors properly, creation does not necessarily lead to progression, it can also bring on regression.

And finally, "Innovation".

The difference between creation and innovation resides in the fact that the latter is the diffusion of creation. Innovation is a creation that gets diffused, multiplied, and propagated, one that diversifies. If we continue with this metaphor of sexual reproduction a little further, human reproduction becomes creation when it frees itself from its parents. Finally, man–creation becomes man–innovation when he multiplies, doesn't remain a unique example, and becomes a parent himself. We have then the repetition of the sexual act, then reproduction, then creation, then innovation.

As we can see, each of the four driving principles is the condition for the others. There are linked. The travel of Transformation utilizes all four of them. The story of institutions, the story of mankind in general, is full of creations that never managed to become innovations or who had to wait for years, decades, even centuries before they could transform into innovations. Leonardo di Vinci, who, amongst other things, had already imagined a helicopter, is the archetype of this delay. For a creation to become innovation, it must be sustained and fed by its technical, social, but also psychic and spiritual environment. In France, there is every year a DIY fair, where genius inventors regularly present numerous creations, but only a handful of them will become innovations. It is actually healthy that they don't all become innovations, otherwise we would be submerged with them, without any possibility of containing them, in other words to contain the anxiety that many of them would generate. Innovation is also a function of its acceptability by its environment. When a company, an institution or a system refuses this reality principle, they become dominated by *crazy entrepreneurs* and are sentencing themselves to regression until they disappear. This links back to a fashionable notion, which is highly justified in this case: the *intelligence of situations*. In other words, taking into account the reality principle, which is regulated either by the death principle or by the pleasure principle, either by *Thanatos* or by *Eros*.

*   *   *

The books that I had brought with me to Ostuni have stayed on the mantelpiece in my hotel room. I haven't had time to consult them and I haven't felt the need to do so. The journey that I have been on up to now with David is completely new. Naturally it was fed by our cultures, but I believe, more importantly, it was also guided by the encounter itself, by the secret alchemy of this long discussion (and writing) at the heart of an

Apulian August. I leave blank the left hand-side of the page in the notepads on which I transcribe the interview with David Gutmann. It is a space for margin annotations, for certain suggestions, and for some invisible ink writing that remains sometimes mute even for my interlocutor. Today, I can't remember about which digression in our conversation, I wrote down a compliment he gave me: "what I like about working with you, is that you bring me onto terrains unknown to me." I think that even Gutmann has already partly modified his manuscript. It is not by chance, as the end of our stay here in Ostuni is nearing, that he comes to our meetings with ideas, which of course, he fears, may vanish in the course of this "loose" discussion. That is not all: the barn has become a kind of branch of "Praxis International" in the deep South. David is asking Paris to fax him page after page of etymological research. The paper roll for the fax machine of this rustic office has run out, it might have lasted the whole season otherwise. This morning the ritual of the jug of water that welcomes us into the garden—two glasses of water, an embroidered linen cloth to protect the jug from insects—was marked by vinegar! Somebody had poured some into the water. Was it a joke? A boycott?

I am tired, at times very tired. During the first hours of the afternoon, straight after the break, I now tend not to drive the seven or eight kilometres that separate me from my hotel. There is too much sun and the break would be too short anyway. I have a rest instead in Raphael's room, affectionately warned, by his dad, with post-its on the door that "your bed is being used by Oscar, who thanks you for your hospitality." I even manage to believe that this accursed book "doesn't exist". I get cross and I allow myself be invaded by Maritè's discouragement. It wasn't an easy encounter. Inadvertently, I almost immediately left behind my "clothes" of professional journalist and exposed myself to the confrontation of another look: Judaism, journey, Transformation.

However "the book does exist" and you are reading it.

Notes

1. French expression for "acting out", literally meaning "missed/failed act".
2. "*Scatole*" means box in Italian, the expression "*rompere le scatole*" is a rude expression meaning "to annoy someone", hence the play on words with "*scatole*".

3. French for fundamentalist.
4. Italian word for emprise.
5. This word also means emprise.

CHAPTER TEN

The zigzags of passion

W e have been saying over the last few days that to desire means to stop looking at the stars and to put one's feet back on the ground so as to be more able to continue on the journey. To desire where to put one's feet and one's eyes on Earth: in that way, the Transformation-Approach, by promoting realism, contributes to the containment of anxiety. It makes it possible, above all to see, and therefore to understand and to interpret. In this approach, regression must be considered as inevitable. In the current Italian political system, Bossi and the Lega Nord, I repeat, constitute an indispensable regression on the country's path to Transformation, a path that is Italy's within the rest of Europe. It was not by chance that the audience booed Bossi during a performance of a Verdi Opera in Verona's arena. Knowing and understanding does not mean depreciating, but, on the contrary, appreciating a little bit better what is at stake. If that perception had been at work at the end of the twenties, they would have understood quicker that the regression with Mussolini was inevitable and therefore still "stoppable". Fortunately, nowadays there are *blockers*: new political figures, Europe. Italy is an open system. After Moro and Mani Pulite, the country transformed and now has more vitality than France.

Let us try to apply the Transformation-Approach to the case of Bossi, shall we?

Certainly. I think that the feeling of regional identity, and in particular for the Italians from the North, has now been sufficiently nourished by Bossi and his Lega's political advent. By that I mean that such an identity will not go as far as secession, Bossi having already faced a series of defeats. The fantasy of separation must precisely remain a fantasy, in contrast to Belgium or Yugoslavia. Isn't Italy's history, after all, one of dialectics between North and South? It is relationship that constantly needs to be rejuvenated through conflict. If we take away one of the two elements, the possibility for transformation does not exist any more. Zigs need zags and *vice versa*. Italy is a country of two tribes, the zigs and the zags: zig cannot exist without zag. Sometimes zig is in power, sometimes he isn't, and reciprocally.

Zigzagging a bit in our conversation, with an apparent methodological anarchy that I very much like, I would like to go from public to private and ask you to follow on from yesterday's conversation, on how we can rehabilitate emotions and affects in everyday life, particularly at work.

You are right to be talking about *emotions* and *affects*, to which I would add *feelings* and *sensations*. For me the *rift*, the irreconcilable separation, the split as the English would say, is amongst the greatest catastrophe. I am not talking about the *split* between private sphere and public sphere (which is not that bad), but of the one that leads to the attribution to the private sphere of anything that has to do with feelings and emotions, and of the devolution, on the other hand, of the public sphere of anything that has to do with rationality, thoughts, and reflections. This is a crime against the human being, a human who experiences within him, simultaneously, emotions and reflections, feelings and thoughts, affects and reasoning, sensations and elaborations. A human cannot understand himself if not through the mobilization of those four couples.

However, can modern and contemporary history, the western one in particular, be "read" as a suppressing of anything that is not produced by rationality?

Yes, or at least as an attempt to suppress. That certainly is the case with institutional life. But, even beyond that, not only have feelings been relegated exclusively to the intimacy of individuals, the couple, the family, but they have been considered—and still are—as belonging to the realm of the inexpressible and unspeakable, if not the ignoble and vile. What a mistake! Because as always, what is not known, recognized or understood at least partially, dominates us, especially when we are not aware of it. How many crucial decisions have been taken, through the course of history, in the different kinds of institution, including companies, in the place of unexpressed feelings! Think about Cleopatra's nose, Napoleon's small height, De Gaulle's destiny marked by his name ...

Can you give us examples drawn from your experience of being a consultant?

One of the leaders of this big High Tech company, also established in Israel, is one of the survivors of the Shoah, the miraculous outcome of a tragedy. In that way he has created and promoted, within his company, a survival culture, which made the company very efficient, but at the cost of constant sacrifices, banishing, and unwise losses. Thus, a part of the company puts itself in great danger because of the impossibility of finding new leaders and new managers to succeed this leader. We are talking here of somebody who has never wanted to process the fact that he survived, and who chooses, certainly not by chance, dangerous leisure activities such as skydiving, aviation, and motorbikes. Here is another example: with a manager who lives within a family, a situation of conflict is almost impossible to work with on Mondays or Tuesdays, straight after the weekend spent with his family. In that way, we can say that every one of us has developed, to quote Eric Berne, a personal *script* through a stock, a specific reserve of emotions, feelings, and affects. Every time that one of these feelings is reactivated, it throws us back to the initial situation and the person's reactions will only have very little to do with the situation in the here and now. Even more so, these feelings and affects create, consciously and strongly, a request for reactivation in each of us. We will, thus, be tempted to transform the here and now, and therefore reality, in order to find again and dive into our primordial situation.

Did you recognize this "script" in your personal history too?

In my personal history, the feeling of abandonment is very strong. It comes from the feeling of abandonment of my father, who "left" his wife and his children and created within me a terror of being abandoned in the way that it happened, in my imaginary, to my father's first family. Indeed, every time in my life, including my professional life, that I had the feeling of being abandoned, I would react in an excessive and very violent way. However, I became aware of something even harder. I unconsciously create situations of abandonment or I put myself in the conditions of being abandoned. It is only when I came to know concretely what had happened in the past, and with the help of the work of psychoanalysis, that I began to understand this situation and, therefore, to come out of such a script. I am not saying this to defend, or even promote psychoanalysis: everyone finds their own specific path of clarification. But it is clear, however, that institutions are both places of repetition for individual and social scripts, and equally places that increase the capacity for elucidation and clarification of these scripts. It is not about doing psychodramas or collective analysis sessions but rather about pushing an institution to comprehend and to be even more efficient, whether it is from an economic or a social perspective.

Let us look, then, at the processing of feelings, at the, for want of a better word, positive part.

The crucial importance in processing feelings, affects, emotions, and sensations does not lie solely in the negative aspect of not processing, since we have already said that if they are not being used, they will become dangerous, destructive, and regressive. There are, also, positive reasons. Using feelings creates additional and complementary sources and resources for the travel of Transformation. These additional sources are *other*: they bring an extremely useful dimension. Indeed, we can find here some of the best boosters. The etymological roots will help us in clarifying this process. *Feeling* comes from the verb to *feel*, which means *to perceive*, feelings are linked to knowledge. In *sensation*, there is a sense[1] of travel and meaning. One must use his senses, and not just his head.

In *affect*, which comes from *afficher*,[2] there is, on the other hand, doing, touching, moving, and inducing: "touching" the state of things to modify it and specifically to bring desire into play and an eagerness for modifying a system. As for *emotion*, the word means putting into motion, leaving a person, an institution, a society, a system that is fixed and paralysed by the unconscious weight of the past in their initial script. The mass of a system, pushing against its resistances, is the first thing that has to be put into motion. It is the same in physics. We know very well that mass is a lot lighter in water. Freedom, in its liquid nature, is a medium that lightens the weight of the mass. Emotion is what shakes, what puts into motion: the motion of the travel of Transformation. Using emotions, feelings, affects, which modern and contemporary western culture has refused to do, pushes you to accept yourself in the movement, in a process of fulfilment that is never ending, but which allows oneself to feel a little bit better amidst the complexity of the human condition. It is not just words but is extremely concrete (as indeed words are!). For example, someone questioning their own professional life at some point, will be able, in a meeting, to ask themselves the following questions: what emotion are they feeling, what sensation are they experiencing, what feeling animates them, what affect touches them? In answering those questions, they will open new horizons, pre-vent, give themselves signs that pure rationality cannot procure them. They even have, before the signs, the opportunity to make visible facts that were hidden. When such a process is accomplished in a participative, shared way, the sources and resources for knowledge and comprehension get multiplied. Heuristic and Hermeneutic—finding and interpreting facts—reveal to us their meaning and their contribution only when an individual or an institution manages to mobilize both rationality and passion.

"Passion" is a new word in your vocabulary. It is coming up here for the first time, after ten days of conversation.

Passion, in fact, comes from the Greek *pateo* which means to walk, to go or to travel through, and from the Latin *passus*, passage. It gave, for example, "path" in English. Passion is what induces freedom, opens the door, and allows the passage. A passion that isn't recognized or used brings about pathos, pain, and suffering.

The passion of Christ is also a path, the path of the cross. Is there a prevalence of Greek and Latin terms?

Indeed, and the different passions, just like affects, not only alternate, but coexist. In an institution in transformation, each sub-system will carry within itself, simultaneously and in parallel, different passions. The articulation of these different passions, shared within the institution, will create the political, psychic, and spiritual states of the institution at each period of its existence. A sub-system, for example, will be carrying more of the fear, whilst another may represent courage. Talent resides in the fact of recognizing both one and the other as resources for the institution.

Is every passion legitimate?

Absolutely. Managing is having the capacity to implement a process of containment of all the different passions. I would even add that every passion is useful because it makes revelation possible. It is revelation itself, like in the Passion of Christ. Accepting the use of passions provokes surprise: it is fabricating surprise that undoes the hold[3]—knowing, as well, that a part of the process of expressing passions happens through dreams. When we say that passions dominate and destroy the world, we are disastrously mistaken. To the contrary, the absence of the bringing into awareness of passions provokes regressive fissures, without condensation, without metaphor and without Transformation. Becoming aware of one's own passions is the most constructive way to use them, so that it is not the passions that end up abusing us, as it is most often the case. I really think to paraphrase Clausewitz, that *war is the displacement of passion by other means*. In fact, passions, when not recognized and not processed, are the source of negative projections. They then become introjections for others, resolving in that way an unconscious demand for projections and their co-substantial acceptance. Therefore, in my personal case that we talked about earlier, when I was repeating a process of abandonment, I was attracting projections of abandonment, by making myself a victim and a scapegoat. In that way, *to be passionate* is the best way *to be reasonable*. The "great transformers", leaders, and managers of societies and companies, are most of the time people who live passionately. They live great passions, they concretely live the passion of Transformation in the eyes of others.

Professor David Gutmann, our interview ends here. Is there a question that I haven't asked you or that you are asking yourself?

No, however there is an anecdote that I would like to tell. My second intervention in Israel in 1987 was designed as a workshop in which a military instructor for fighting pilots, a top gun, took part. At the end of the workshop, this officer came to me and told me whilst imitating my French accent: "Mister Gutmann, you are just like Inspector Clouzot". Why? I asked him. He then said: "you never do the same mistake twice, because you always find a new one to make!" So there you have it, the Transformation-Approach is not about repeating the same mistake, it is about always finding a new one to live ...

*   *   *

It's over. There is the taste of a holiday ending, a vague sadness that descends when you are just about to go home. Tomorrow morning David and his family will have gone back to Paris. We have dinner together, and I end up smoking the half cigar that David offered me several days ago. On the esplanade of the fortified barn we say goodbye. I walk down the open path that leads to the street. At the junction, out of the blue, I start crying. This may seem rhetorical and stupid, but that's how it was. In my hotel, in the middle of the night, there is complete silence. Unexpectedly a fawn appears, straight out of nowhere, God knows why. We are on a hill, a few kilometres from the sea. But animals are "miracles", by that I mean that they are, from now on, the rarest of epiphanies to which personally I am now learning to give meaning: as if a caveman had seen a car!

That evening I asked David why he had wanted to do this book with me, and to do it even when someone close to him thought that it would be better to go to a French journalist. He said that he had "felt" straight away in me that I was a man without any prejudice of any kind; ethnic, religious or cultural. It is one of the most beautiful compliments anyone has ever given me. David Gutmann also put himself on the spot. He drove his family here and he ventured into a frank and detailed synthesis of his pragmatic itinerary, relying on me to transcribe this "writing of the praxis", which carried him to a territory mostly yet unexplored.

Our relationship was not "all rosy". There was and there will be contradictions and regressions. But David Gutmann truly arrived at a time in my life when it was simply necessary that something absolutely unprecedented happened, something past and something to come. We wrote together a book that won't change anyone's life, but which, perhaps, will be able to help the reader in the deciding passages in the book of their life, those "passages of passion".

Notes

1. The Latin etymological roots of *sense* and *sensation* are better preserved in French, where *sens* also means direction, way.
2. French for, to advertise, to make clear.
3. In French: la prise.

Glossary of transformation

Anxiety: Anxiety is in relation to death and is, therefore, physiological. The management of anxiety is most delicate and it includes depression as well as creativity. Creativity frees itself and bursts out of anxiety when the latter is no longer submitted to, but managed, contained, and transformed.

Blocker: A protection mechanism, which is set off to block regression. The term is borrowed from computer science, and was first used after the New York stock exchange crash in October 1987.

Black box: A metaphorical representation of the Unconscious. We don't know everything and we can't know everything. There is a black box beyond our Conscious, in which certain things—fortunately—remain invisible. The black box is an antidote to the temptation of omnipotence, to the emprise of the Prometheus myth. If we attempt to open the black box, in other words if we try to know everything, the black box then becomes Pandora's box, which will release a great number of evils. What will come out of it then, is mostly totalitarian thinking and ill from omnipotence and omniscience, because understanding the world is impossible. It is rather an attempt to dominate it and to reify it. However, it is possible to reduce the volume of the black box through a constant attempt at sharing interpretations and their consecutive choices.

Transparent box or glass box: Symbolizes the subconscious. It is the box through which the limited, temporal, tormented passage from the Unconscious to the Conscious, from unconscious to conscious, occurs. The transparent box, if it is not engaged in a Transformation process, encloses and isolates us. We see it and we don't see it: the elements are often visible, comprehensible, but we do not see them, because if we did we would be forced to act accordingly.

Booster: Represents a mechanism that promotes progression. The word comes from North American popular language and is used in the aerospace industry or in advertising. To boost means to "launch" missiles, a product or an actor. Boosters are first and foremost mechanisms, processes, and individuals who speed up or re-launch the progression phases in Transformation.

Buffer: A mechanism that prevents individual or social progression, but which can also slow down regression. The word also means "shield, plug" when borrowed from the automotive and railway industry. In a company, bureaucrats are *buffers*, just as the very culture of the company is a buffer. When it slows down the race of those unstoppable entrepreneurs, "the crazy entrepreneurs", who risk bringing the company to ruin, this mechanism is sometimes a positive one. Buffers belong to the realm of repetition and can, therefore, prevent harmful excesses.

Conflict: Represents the foundation of democracy, because any life is conflicted. It is out of the confrontation produced by contradictions that a new stage in Transformation can be born.

Containment: An essential quality of the human condition that supports and reveals the Transformation of roles, relationships, systems, resistances, and projections.

Creativity: Creativity does not exist without the continual exchange with the other, with the environment, be it of an institution, a company or a symbolic language. It derives from the management and containment of anxiety.

Democracy: The practice of Transformation is a process of learning about democracy. It is a permanent and unsatisfactory search which does not ignore, or even recognize, that the state of the nature of individuals and systems lead to death. Democracy is, in psychic terms, the opposite of a phantasy of immortality at work in nations, institutions, and companies. It is, therefore, the awareness of finitude and imperfection and the necessity for the other.

Experience: Carries the praxis of Transformation and necessitates the others. It helps in containing anxiety and finding the way through, beyond more and more narrow paths of regressions. It makes it possible to escape the danger of exclusive and mortifying repetition.

Faith: A secular accepting of oneself and one's future. Faith that resistances will give in and that only a society in transformation can and must also be nurturing.

Feelings: A crucial resource in the Transformation-Approach and a source of knowledge and action. Rarely utilized by western rationality, which precisely tried to exorcize them.

Freedom: Freedom resides in the flow from unconscious to conscious. It has a liquid origin (liberty), the Greek root *lib*, which it also shares with desire, with *libido*.

Here and now: The very dimension of Transformation.

Hybrid: The closest concept to the reality of the other; not a synthesis, but a third way or form, different from that of the two genitor-elements that meet (even though certain characteristics remain common to both).

Institutional Transformation: An intervention of advice, which involves working with a group, institution or company in a similar way that a psychotherapist would see a patient, in a synthetic dimension but without considering them as "ill". Institutional Transformation (IT) differs from the so-called Organizational Development (OD) or Human Resources (HR) movements by its ambition to take into consideration, whenever possible, the unconscious and its expressions. In order to discover and interpret unconscious processes in institutions, the focus of attention is placed on the exercising of authority and on leadership. The unconscious, once revealed, and when it is understood at least partially by members of the institution, can indeed become a resource. The work of IT is concerned with the transformation of roles, relations, projections, resistances, and systems. It constitutes a real Transformation-Approach of reality.

Interpretation: Interpreting is fundamental to being able to choose in relative freedom and to act consequently. Every choice carries with it suffering, because choosing involves discerning, renouncing, and giving up. Governing and self-governing means interpreting in order to choose. The capacity for *inter*-preting reduces the distance between self and others.

In-the-mind (ghetto, prison, consultant, manager … in-the-mind): An archaic psychic resistance that prevents the emergence of interpretations in reality, but which, once transformed, becomes a quality that anyone can value—with others—in their daily work.

Journey: Represents the matrix of experience and the confrontation of reality. It is the travel of transformation in its realization, with the vicissitudes, the meanders, and the zigzags unique to each learning process. The journey makes each of us a protagonist.

Leadership: A leader generates ideas, actions, other leaders, and successors. Successors rather than passive disciples who must act simultaneously, after, and against him are crucial in leadership. A leader must also be a container for projections, capable of embanking them consciously, to process them and transform them.

Living: Life only exists in its relation to death. Those who live fully and consciously are those individuals or systems with the capacity to recognize that one day they will disappear. Living is accepting the passing of time—in other words Transformation—the travel from one state to another, with other people.

Management: Represents the capacity to offer and to establish the conditions and the resources so that others can be managers of themselves. Politically, management is truly joint management; psychically, management is the fact of containing fears, uncertainties, and especially anxieties that go with the search for freedom in a process of Transformation.

Mourning: Mourning is the archetype of Transformation. It is its matrix, for individuals as well as communities. Not processing mourning leads to depression. There is a depression of systems that prevents their healthy functioning and darkens their future. To negate death is the surest way of triggering it.

Other: A constituent of the Ego, of the personal identity. Without the relation to the other, Transformation is not possible. Indeed, the latter is a process that necessitates co-authors.

Passage: The symbol of Transformation at work. The nearer we get to a passage, the stronger the increase of the *resistances* that want to bring us back to the initial order. Any process of Institutional Transformation, including psychoanalysis, is "successful" only if the act of passage that they represent prevents the acting out.

Passion: In the journey of Transformation, passion is the bearer of freedom that proclaims decisive passages. If it is not recognized and utilized, passion produces pain and pathos.

Projection: In psychoanalysis, it is a mechanism by which we displace onto another what we don't like, what we can't bear within ourselves (feelings, fantasies, faults), in order to allegedly get rid of it or free ourselves from it. Projections are dangerous for self and others, especially when they are not recognized as such and are, therefore, not processed. When, in an institution, an individual or a sub-system recognizes and takes back its own projections, we are in the presence of an institution in Transformation. Transformation is, in fact, first and foremost, a transformation of projections.

Project: A matrix of projections, which generates and attracts other projections. A project is an open invitation to fantasies or even madness, because the fantasies at work cannot be regulated any more within the projections, within the denial of reality. However, a project for a nation, a company or a person—as a landmark against uncertainty—is positive so long as it does not become definitive, absolute, and totalitarian.

Regression: Regression is the death principle in action. It promotes the prevalence of Thanatos in its alliance with madness and splitting. It can be either an individual schizophrenia, or an extreme social fragmentation. Regression is suffering for the sake of suffering and a flight from the principle of reality. Knowing that in our life there will be regressions makes it possible to lighten our feelings of guilt, because often a regression allows the arrival of a *progression*. The role of the consultant, with a manager, is to detect as soon as possible when and how a regression has started, in order to act, and to stop it as quickly as possible.

Revelation: It is important to seek to reveal the *hic et nunc*, the here and now, not only through the psychoanalytic insight, but also through the inputs, which make the outputs possible. It is about revealing, in order to transform. Revelation is never a solitary labour, but shared between the analyst and the patient, or between the consultant and the "consultee". Any true revelation is dialectic.

Rugby: The oval shape of a rugby ball renders its trajectories unpredictable. It becomes the ball of anti-omnipotence, the rebounding ball of Transformation. Furthermore, in rugby, the "transformation"[1] of the try increases the score!

Saviour: There is no saviour. A saviour is an idol. This role must be refused, because in taking it on we inevitably enter a vicious circle: the saviour quickly becomes either a persecutor and, therefore, a victim, or a victim and then a persecutor. What gets established is a vicious circle "S.V.P.". Every process of rescuing an institution is bound to fail right from the start.

Script: In the language of Transactional Analysis, founded by Eric

Berne, the "script" is that childhood scenario which—under the condition of the combination of certain circumstances—imposes, every time, the same behaviour, loyal to the role carried or imposed precisely in childhood. Freedom is the emergency exit or the giving up of the script. There is an institutional script at work in systems.

Surviving: The extreme experience of Nazi camps or of terminally ill people. But you can also find it in the "banal" existence that does not take into account the passing of time, by trying to suspend it or to annihilate it. It is a daily suffering whose goal is to, everyday, repeat the previous one.

Void: Lack or vacuum are accepted because they allow creation. "In the beginning there was void", the *Talmud* says. "Without memory or desire": it is in that way, according to W. R. Bion, that every psychoanalysis session should start, at least for the analyst.

Zigzags: They incarnate Transformation's way of proceeding, between regressions and progressions, between destructions and constructions, to create a journey that is built through journeying. Their alternating offers an alternative to either the impasse derived from the fact of going "round" in circles, or to the fantasy of omnipotence inherent to the itinerary of the always "straight ahead" characteristic of the myth of Progress.

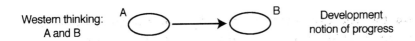

Western thinking: A and B development, notion of progress.

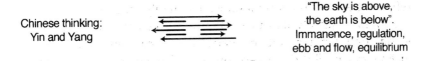

Chinese thinking: Yin and Yang "the sky is above, the earth is below" immanence, regulation, ebb and flow, equilibrium.

Transformation:
Zig and Zag

A ... B

The journey matters
more than the aim,
to regressions
progressions succeed

Transformation: Zig and Zag the journey matters more than the aim, to regressions progressions succeed.

Note

1. In French rugby, the conversion that follows a try is called "transformation".

Selected reading

GUTMANN David (with) IARUSSI Oscar

*La Trasformazione. Psicoanalisi, desidero e management nelle organiz-
zazioni.* Salerno: Edizioni Sottotraccia, 1999.

La Transformation. Psychanalyse, désir et management. Lyon: L'Hermès,
2000.

TERNIER-DAVID Jacqueline

L'entreprise dans la crise italienne. Paris: Masson, Collection Institut de
l'Entreprise, 1982.

GUTMANN David

*Pouvoir et Autorité. Lettre de la Société Internationale des Conseillers de
Synthèse,* 1–10. Paris, décembre 1983.

The Decline of Traditional Defences against Anxiety. Proceedings of the
First International Symposium on Group Relations, Keeble College,
Oxford, 5–22. Washington: A. K. Rice, 1989; *Notes du Conjoncture
Sociale,* 342, 18–31. Paris, juin 1990.

*De L'Agglomération à la cité formation et trans-formation de la ville.
Vers une nouvelle culture urbaine.* Les Rencontres de Marne-la-Vallée,
135–156. Altamira: Epamarne/Epafrance, 1993.

Reduction in the Effectiveness of Social Systems as a Defence Against Anxiety. Career development World-wide: "How to Learn from each other". In *Journal of Career Development*, 20 (1). USA, 1993.

GUTMANN David and PIERRE Ronan
Consultation and Transformation: Between shared Management and Generative Leadership. In E. B. Klein, F. Gabelnick and P. Herr (Eds.), *Dynamic Consultation in a Changing Workplace*, 3–31. Madison, CT: Psychosocial Press, 2000.

GUTMANN David and PONTHIEU Laurence
Transformation du langage, transformation sociale. Proceedings of the International Conference "At the Threshold of the Millennium", vol. I, 150–153. Lima: SIDEA & PromPeru, 1999.

GUTMANN David, PIERRE Ronan, TERNIER-DAVID Jacqueline and VERRIER Christophe
Los caminos de la autoridad: del más acá al más allá. Intervención en la Universidad Arabe de Jerusalém. Perspectivas de Gestion, 2, 5–13. Barcelona, 1997.
The Paths of Authority: From the Unconscious to the Transcendental. Intervention at the Arab University of Jerusalem. In F. Avallone, J. Arnold and K. de Witte (Eds.), *Feelings work in Europe*, 172–181. Milan: Guerini, 1997.
Die Wege der Autorität: vom Unbewussten zum Transzendentalen: Intervention an der Arabischen Universität von Jerusalem. Organisationsentwicklung, 1, 4–13. Basel, 1998.

GUTMANN David, TERNIER-DAVID Jacqueline and VERRIER Christophe
Gruppe Og Transformation (Groups and Transformation). Ubevidste Processer: Organisation Og Ledelse, 171–181. Copenhagen: Dansk Industri, February 1995.
Paradoxer och förvandling I konsultrollen: Fran reparation till uppenbareise (Paradox and Transformation playing Consultants: from Repairing to Revelation). In S. B. Boëthius and S. Jern (Eds.), *Den svarfangade organisationen*, 133–160. Stockholm: Natur och Kultur, 1996.

Transformation et collusion. De la conformation à l'alliance. *Insight*, 3 (décembre). Bari, Italie, 1996; *Management et Conjoncture Sociale*, 507, 9–23. Paris, avril 1997.

From Envy to Desire: Witnessing the Transformation. In R. French and R. Vince (Eds.), *Group Relations, Management, and Organisation*, 155–172. Oxford: Oxford University Press, 1999.

BERMAN Avi, BERGER Miriam and GUTMANN David
The Division into Us and Them as a Universal Social Structure. Mind and Human Interaction, 11(1) (Trauma & Identity), 53–72. Connecticut: International Universities Press, Inc, 2000; In S. Ostroff (Ed.), *Dialogue and Leadership across the Faultlines of Israeli Society: Developing Theory and Practice*, 305–328. Jerusalem: The Joint-Brookdale Institute, 2000, (Hebrew).